Faik Konitza
1876-1942

To Eddie McParland

Faik Konitza

Selected Correspondence

Edited by
Bejtullah Destani

Introduction by
Robert Elsie

To Gabriel,
from Bejtullah
01.07.2002
London

The Centre for Albanian Studies,
London

FIRST EDITION
Published December 2000 by
The Centre for Albanian Studies

Distributed by
Learning Design, English Street, London E3 4TA
Tel: 020 8983 1944 Fax: 020 8983 1932
e-mail: info@learningdesign.org
website: www.learningdesign.org

ISBN 1 873928 18 1

Contents

Introduction by Robert Elsie page vii

'Faik Bey Konitza' by Guillaume Apollinaire,
'Mercure de France', 1st May 1912 page 1

1. Faik Konitza to Devish Bey Elbasani page 6
2. Faik Konitza to & from W.E. Gladstone page 10
3. Faik Konitza to Theodor Ippen page 12
4. Faik Konitza to Baron Goluchowski page 14
5. Faik Konitza to Baron Goluchowski page 18
6. Faik Konitza to Baron Goluchowski page 22
7. Faik Konitza to Viosarion Dodani page 25
8. Faik Konitza to Visarion Dodani page 26
9. Faik Konitza to Visarion Dodani. page 28
10. Faik Konitza to Visarion Dodani page 29
11. Faik Konitza to Visarion Dodani page 31
12. Faik Konitza to Visarion Dodani page 32
13. Faik Konitza to Shahin Bey Kolonja page 34
14. To the Albanians by Faik Konitza page 37
15. Faik Konitza to Kristo Qiriazi page 38
16. Faik Konitza to Kristo Floqi page 40
17. Faik Konitza to Theodor Ippen page 41
18. Faik Konitza to Lef Nosi page 47
19. Faik Konitza to the Chairman of 'Bashkimi Society' page 48
20. Faik Konitza to Nikolla Ivanaj page 50
21. Faik Konitza to Nikolla Ivanaj page 51
22. Faik Konitza to Nikolla Ivanaj page 53
23. Faik Konitza to Lef Nosi page 54
24. Faik Konitza to Dervish Bey Elbasani page 55
25. Faik Konitza to Lef Nosi page 56
26. Faik Konitza to The Foreign Office page 58
27. Faik Konitza to Aubrey Herbert page 61
28. Faik Konitza to Aubrey Herbert page 62
29. Faik Konitza to Aubrey Herbert page 63

30. Faik Konitza to Aubrey Herbert page 65
31. Faik Konitza to Professor Hans Delbruck page 66
32. Faik Konitza to Parashqevi Qiriazi page 73
33. Faik Konitza to Dervish Bey Elbasani page 74
34. Faik Konitza to Dervish Bey Elbasani page 78
35. Faik Konitza to Aubrey Herbert page 81
36. Faik Konitza to the Chairman of 'Vatra' page 82
37. Faik Konitza to Aubrey Herbert page 85
38. 'The Telephone Invasion of Albania' by Faik Konitza page 87
39. Faik Konitza to the editor of the New York Times page 90
40. To Messrs Dervish Duma & Anton Logoreci page 94
41. Faik Konitza to Dervish Duma page 96
42. Sumner Welles to Faik Konitza page 98
43. Dervish Duma to Faik Konitza page 100
44. Dervish Duma to Faik Konitza page 118
45. Faik Konitza to Dervish Duma page 121
46. Dervish Duma to Faik Konitza page 124
47. Faik Konitza to Sotir Martini page 128
48. Faik Konitza to Sotir Martini page 129
49. Faik Konitza to Sotir Martini page 130
50. Faik Konitza to Sotir Martini page 134
51. Faik Konitza to King Zog page 131
52. Faik Konitza to Sotir Martini page 133
53. Faik Konitza to Sotir Martini page 134
54. Faik Konitza to King Zog page 136
55. The Last Hours of Konitza page 138
56. Charlotte Graham to Sotir Martini page 142
57. Memoramdum to the Foreign Ministry of Austro-Hungarian Empire by Faik Konitza page 144
58. Funeral Oration of Faik Konitza by Bishop F.S. Noli page 174

Notes page 177
Index page 183
Acknowledgements page 185

Introduction

by Robert Elsie

Faik bey Konitza (1876-1942) was one of the great figures of Albanian intellectual culture in the early decades of the twentieth century and was no doubt the first Albanian whom one might consider to have been a real European.

Konitza was born on 15 March 1876 in Konitsa, then in Albania and now part of Greece in the Pindus mountains, not far from the present Albanian border. After elementary schooling in Turkish in his native village, he studied at the Jesuit Saverian College in Shkodra which offered him not only some instruction in Albanian but also an initial contact with central European culture and Western ideas. From there, he continued his schooling at the French-language Imperial Galata secondary school in Constantinople. In 1890, at the age of fifteen, he was sent to study in France where he spent the next seven years. After initial education at secondary schools in Lisieux (1890) and Carcassonne (1892), he registered at the University of Dijon, from which he graduated in 1895 in Romance philology. After graduation, he moved to Paris for two years where he studied mediaeval French, Latin and Greek at the Collége de France. He finished his studies at Harvard University in the United States, although little is known of this period of his life. As a result of his highly varied educational background, he was able to speak and write Albanian, Italian, French, German, English and Turkish fluently.

Konitza's stay in France, a country of long-standing liberal democratic traditions, was to have a profound effect on him and he was able to acquire and adopt the patterns of Western thinking as no Albanian intellectual had ever done before him. The young Konitza was particularly marked by the uninhibited freedom which the French press enjoyed in the years of open and caustic debate sparked by the Dreyfus affair. It was during this period that he began to take an interest in his native language and his country's history and literature, and to write articles on Albania for a French newspaper.

In September 1897 he moved to Brussels, where at the age of twenty-two he founded the periodical *'Albania'*, which was soon to become the most important organ of the Albanian press at the turn of the century. He moved to London in 1902 and continued to publish the journal there until 1909.

It was in London that Konitza made friends with the noted French poet and critic Guillaume Apollinaire (1880-1918), initially through correspondence on an article published by the poet in 1903 in *'L'Europèen'*. Apollinaire stayed with Konitza at the latter's Chingford home in 1903 and 1904 while endeavouring to regain the affections of his beloved Annie Playden. Konitza not only hosted the poet, but seems also to have served as an intermediary in the *'affaire de coeur'* Contacts between the two writers were finally lost in 1909 when Konitza emigrated to the United States. Apollinaire endeavoured to find the Albanian publisher there, but received no response to his letters.

Konitza's first stop in the New World was Boston where he became editor of the Albanian-language newspaper *'Dielli' (The Sun)*, *'Dielli'* was the organ of the important Pan-Albanian *'Vatra' (The Hearth)* Federation of Boston, of which Konitza became general secretary in 1912. He also edited one other short-lived periodical: the Boston weekly *'Flamuri' (The Banner)* in 1910 and the fortnightly *'Trumbeta e Krujës' (The Trumpet of Croya)* in St Louis, Missouri, which he ran for a short time (three editions) in 1911. In 1912 he travelled to London on behalf of the *'Vatra'* federation to defend Albania's interests at the Conference of Ambassadors. This conference, held in the autumn of that year, was to consider recognition of the fledgling Albanian state which had declared its independence from the Ottoman Empire on 28 November. On 17 December 1912, the ambassadors agreed to recognize Albanian autonomy, though initially under the continued suzerainty of the Sultan. At the beginning of March 1913, Konitza, who had quarrelled with Ismail Qemal bey Vlora (1844-1919) and initially given his support to the government of Esad Pasha Toptani (1863-1920), also was elected as President of the the Albanian Congress of Trieste who had gathered to discuss their country's fate during the political anarchy precipitated by the Balkan Wars. He became disillusioned with Austro-Hungarian policies, which he had earlier supported, when it became clear that Vienna was only interested in a fixed northern border for Albania and that his native town of Konitsa was to be

There, in the political tension created by the war, rumour spread that he was spying for Italy and he was obliged to leave the crumbling Austro-Hungarian Empire for neutral Switzerland. In Lausanne, he met up with Mehdi bey Frashëri (1874-1963) and Mid'hat bey Frashëri (1880-1949), and on 2 November 1915 published a treatise entitled *L'Allemagne et l'Albanie* (Germany and Albania), in which he attacked German support for a proposal to partition Albania between the Greeks and Slavs. In March 1916 we find him in Sofia with Dervish Hima (1873-1928) and in July of that year he was back in Baden (Austria). He was subsequently obliged to leave Austria once again, this time for Italy, because of his criticism of Austrian and German policies in Albania and the consequent suspicion with which the Austrian authorities treated him. In 1921, back in the United States, he was elected president of the *Vatra* federation in Boston and resumed editing the n newspaper *'Dielli' (The Sun)* there, in which he now had his own column, *Shtylla e Konitzës* (Konitza's Column). In the summer of 1926, Faik Konitza was appointed Albanian ambassador to the United States, a post he held until the Italian invasion of his country over Easter 1939. He died in Washington on 15 December 1942 and was buried in Forest Hills cemetery in Boston. After the fall of the Communist dictatorship, his remains were transferred to Tirana in 1995 and interred in a park at the edge of the city.

Faik Konitza wrote little in the way of literature per se, but as a stylist, critic, publicist and political figure he had a tremendous impact on Albanian writing and on the culture of his time. His periodical *Albania*, published in French and Albanian under the pseudonym *Thrank Spirobeg*, not only helped make Albanian culture and the Albanian cause known in Europe, but also set the pace for literary prose in southern Albanian dialect. It is widely considered to be the most significant Albanian periodical to have existed up to the Second World War. Writers like Thimi Mitko (1820-1890), Kostandin Kristoforidhi (1830-1895), Andon Zako Çajupi (1866- 1930) and Gjergj Fishta (1871-1940) first became known to a broader public through the pages of the periodical which Faik Konitza published faithfully over the course of twelve years. *Albania*, financed to some extent by the Austro-Hungarian authorities under the auspices of the *Kultusprotektorat* and accordingly betraying pro-Austrian proclivities, contained articles and information on a wide range of topics: history, language, literature, folklore, archeology, politics, economics, religion and art, and as such constitutes a mini-encyclopaedia of Albanian culture of the period. Konitza valued a free exchange of ideas and he placed the columns of *'Albania'* at the disposal of his rivals whom he countered with caustic wit. In literature, he attacked the often banal nationalist outpourings on the lofty virtues of the Albanian people and called for a more realistic and critical stance towards his nation with all its failings. Steeped in Western culture, he found it difficult to appreciate the poets of early romantic nationalism like Naim bey Frashëri (1846-1900) whose ideals were those of a bygone age and whose verse he regarded as unsophisticated. How could they, with their sacrosanct expressions of patriotic fervour, compare with the higher level of literary and artistic achievement he had encountered in France, to writers like Verlaine, Baudelaire and Apollinaire? The biting sarcasm with which he expressed his intransigence towards the naivety of his compatriots and towards the many sacred cows of Albanian culture and history let a breeze of fresh air into Albanian letters.

Konitza strove for a more refined Western culture in Albania, but he also valued his country's traditions. He was, for instance, one of the first to propagate the idea of editing the texts of older Albanian literature. In an article entitled *'Për Themelimin e Një Gjuhës Letrarishte Shqip' (On the Foundation of an Albanian Literary Language)*, published in the first issue of *'Albania'*, Konitza also pointed to the necessity of creating a unified literary language. He suggested the most obvious solution, that the two main dialects, Tosk and Geg, should be fused and blended gradually. His own fluid style was highly influential in the refinement of southern Albanian Tosk prose writing, which decades later was to form the basis of the modern Albanian literary language (*gjuha letrare*). Konitza's ties with the Zogu regime in later years created consternation among many Albanian intellectuals and it is this more than anything which caused his influence on Albanian literature and culture to be underestimated and ignored by post-war critics in Tirana. His sarcastic comments and polemics in *'Albania'* and elsewhere, and his irascibility and arrogance did not always make him a popular figure, but the spontaneity and refinement of his prose are universally recognized and admired.

Faik Konitza's writings are nonetheless fragmentary. He was the author of numerous editorials and articles on politics, language, literature and history which appeared for the most part in *'Albania e Vogël'* (Little Albania), a fortnightly supplement to his periodical *'Albania'* from 1899 to 1903, He also wrote what could be regarded as a novel, although he never completed it. This is the satirical *'Dr. Gjëlpëra Zbulon Rënjët e Dramës Së Mamurrasit' (Dr Needle Discovers the Roots of the Mamurrasi Drama)* in which he makes some delightfully pungent observations on the backwardness and the questionable hygienic standards of his compatriots. Konitza's only book publication in Albanian was a translation of Arabic tales from a Thousand and One Nights, entitled *Nën hien e hurmave*, Boston 1924 (In the Shade of the Date Palms). In *'Dielli' (The Sun)* from 1929 on, he also edited the narrative of his travels to Albania, a series entitled *'Shqiperia si m'u-duk' (How Albania Appeared to Me)*, in which he expressed much unflattering criticism of various character types he had encountered there: bureaucrats, social climbers, pretentious aristocrats etc. It is only in very recent years that his writings in Albanian have been collected and published. In English, a selection of his work was edited by Qerim M. Panarity in the 175-page volume *'Albania, the Rock Garden of South Eastern Europe and Other Essays*,' Boston 1957.

The present publication, bringing together not only the first English translation of Guillaume Apollinaire's short essay on Konitza, but also much of the Albanian publicist's previously inaccessible correspondence with noted figures of his age, constitutes a further achievement and another step major forward in making this much neglected figure known to the Western reader.

Robert Elsie
Olzheim/Eifel, Germany
Autumn 2000

Faik Bey Konitza

by Guillaume Apollinaire

Mercure de France,

1st May 1912

translated from the French by Andrea Lesic

Of the people I have met and whom I remember with the greatest pleasure, Faik Bey Konitza is one of the most unusual. He was born in Albania some forty years ago, in a family which stayed true to its Catholic faith. This Albanian ['Chkipe'] was raised in France, and when he was about twenty years old, he was so religious that he wanted to enter the Grande Chartreuse monastery as a novice. He did not do it after all, and, bit by bit, his faith turned not so much into indifference, but into a kind of determined anti-clericalism which reminds one a bit of Mérimée's. He continued his studies, but as his was a highly developed love for his fatherland Albania, he returned to Turkey and took part in a conspiracy there, and, according to his own words, was sentenced to death twice in his absence. He went back to France, whose language and literature he knew so well, and got in contact with all those who cared for Albania. However, as the freedoms which exist here did not seem enough to him, he settled in Brussels, in the rue d'Albanie, in order to found a scholarly journal, Albania, which dealt with politics, but even more with literature, history and philology. In this way he devoted much of his life to the Albanian movement; purifying the Albanian language of all unsuitable and parasitic expressions which had slipped into it. In a few years he had turned a rough idiom of sailors' inns into a beautiful, rich and supple language.

However, freedom as it is understood in Brussels was no more to his liking than the Parisian variety. Once he even had to deal with a gendarme in the street, who asked him: *'Your nationality?' - 'I am from Albania.' - 'Where do you live?' - 'In rue d'Albanie -'What do you do?' - 'I edit Albania.' – 'Are you trying to make fun of me?'* asked the gendarme, and the Albanian patriot had to spend that night in the police station. Since he had already had enough of Brussels, Faik Bey Konitza went to London. He left his familiar printer's office, which had only Plantin's typeface and in which he had composed and printed small works, and which today are extremely rare. This had not lasted for long for, working all alone, he had managed one day to mix up all the letters, making them impossible to use any more.

It was in London that I met Faik Bey Konitza, in 1903. He lived in Oakley Crescent, City Road, E.C. I had never met him before. He invited me to spend a few days at his home, and he was supposed to meet me at the station. I needed a sign by which to recognise him, so it was a agreed that he would put an orchid in his lapel. My train arrived very late, and on the platform of Victoria Station all of the gentlemen I saw there had orchids in their lapels. How was I supposed to recognise my Albanian? I took a cab and arrived at his place just as he was going out to buy an orchid.

My stay in London was exceptionably pleasant. Faik Bey Konitza had a passion for the clarinet, oboe and cor anglais. In his drawing room he had an antique collection of these instruments made out of wood. In the morning, while waiting for lunch which was always late, my host would play me old nasal melodies, seated, his eyes cast down, serious, in front of the music stand.

We would have lunch the Albanian way, which is to say, endlessly. Every other day we would have an egg cream, which I did not like at all, and which he thoroughly enjoyed, and the next day we would have a blancmange, which I loved and he never ate.

'The lunches were so long that I could not visit a single museum in London, as we would always arrive when the doors closed.

'However, we went for long walks, and I had the opportunity to see what a sophisticated and fine mind Faik Bey Konitza had. Like all high-born Albanians, he was a bit of a hypochondriac, and I was all the more moved by the friendship which he showed towards me as I saw that his nature was not particularly generous in that respect. His hypochondria was of a very curious kind. If he went to a shop to buy something, he was always afraid that the shopkeeper would run outside after him claiming that he had been robbed. *'Well,'* he would add, *'how would I prove that I had not stolen the thing I had bought?'*

When I saw him in London, he had just completed a major review of his library; he had sold all of his books in order to buy special English editions whose letters are so small that they have to be read with a magnifying glass. Thus he created a new library, quite large, which could all fit into a small cupboard.

Of his old books, he kept only the Dictionary of Pierre Bayle, whom he had chosen as his mentor, and the one by Darmesteter. His greatest literary admiration was for Mr. Remy de Gourmont, and he was very grateful when I later sent him one of his portraits. Faik Bey Konitza, just like that other Bayle, has always had a mania for pseudonyms. He changes them very often. At the time when I knew him, he called himself Thrank Spirobeg, which is the name of the hero of a historical novel by Léon Cahun, a true masterpiece and the best book ever to have been inspired by the history of the Albanians. Having seen, however, that typographers always spelt his pseudonym as Thrank-Spiroberg, Faik Bey Konitza soon decided to adopt it as such.

This lasted only for two or three years; then he took another pseudonym, Pyrrhus Bardyli, which he used for another rich and well written work, entitled *'Essai sur Les Langues Arificielles.'*

I spent some time with Faik Bey Konitza in London on another occasion; he had got married in the meantime and was living in Chingford. It was spring; we used to go for long country walks and spend hours watching golf. A short time before my arrival he had bought some hens, in order to have a ready supply of fresh eggs; but now that he had them, it was impossible for him to eat them, for how can a man eat the eggs of the hens which he knows and feeds himself?

Before long, the hens started to eat their own eggs, which scared Faik Bey Konitza to such an extent that he looked at the poor hens with horror, not daring any more to let them out of the small chicken coop, where they soon killed and ate each other, except for one, who, as she was the victor, remained in solitude for a while. And that one I saw. She became fierce and mad; and, as she was black and skinny, she soon started to look like a crow. Before I left she lost all her feathers, and resembled some kind of rat.

Faik Bey Konitza took a lot of care in editing *'Albania'*. On the cover there was the coat of arms of the future kingdom of Albania, which was designed by a talented French sculptor whose name I forget, and who died a few years ago somewhere near New York in a ballooning accident. However, the attention with which Faik Bey Konitza edited his articles and his slow manner of doing so meant that the journal always came out very late. In 1904, only the issues for the 1902 appeared; in 1907, the issues for 1904 came out at regular intervals.The French journal *'L'Occident'* is the only one which could compete with *'Albania'* in that respect.

When the Turkish revolution started, Faik Bey Konitza thought of returning to his homeland. But events did not turn out as he had hoped. So he decided to go to America at the time when the Albanian rebellion was under way.

He wrote to me for the last time before he left, and after that I never heard from him again. I knew that there was an important and rich Albanian community in America and I believe they extended a warm welcome to the renovator of the Albanian language. I was sorry that he did not keep me informed of his adventures, and then, last year, I found in a bookshop the first issue of the publication *'Trumbeta e Krujës'*, i.e. *'The Trumpet of Kruja,'* which was the capital during Skanderbeg's reign. I saw from it that Faik Bey Konitza was living in St Louis, Missouri, and that he had stopped writing in French, which he knew very well, and had started using English, which he spoke very badly. I wrote to him in St Louis, but I received no reply until a recent letter from Chicago reminded me of my Albanian.

The letter was from a certain 'Benjamin de Caseres', but the handwriting on the envelope left me in no doubt, as it was the handwriting of Faik Bey Konitza. The letters were small and nicely shaped, the 'a' similar to a printed one – he modelled his handwriting on Petrarch's.

I opened the letter. There was a sort of printed, two-page prospectus inside, written in English, entitled *'Prelude'* and dedicated to all those who have been repulsed by my militant egotism. It was a sort of prose poem, full of philosophical sentences and biblical images, in which Beethoven and Goethe were mentioned. This unusual farewell gift, sent by Faik Bey Konitza to all those whom he has known, and with whom he has decided to sever all friendly relations, leaves me in no hope of ever seeing him again.

He has abandoned Europe, he is not publishing *'The Trumpet of Kruja,'* any more, maybe he has even lost interest in *'Albania'*, and now among the business people of Michigan this descendant of the knights of George Kastriot lives with the melancholy of a highly educated European and disillusioned poet, with the hypochondria of an exile and, undoubtedly, with the four large volumes of Bayle's dictionary.

The Letters

[1] Paris, 18 April 1896

translated from the French by Peter Rennie

To Dervish Bey Elbasani

Dear Friend,

I have received your fine letter and I thank you profusely. Unfortunately, I see that you have not understood my thoughts; but the fault is neither yours nor mine, it is our poor language which lacks general and philosophical terms so that it is not possible to express oneself with sufficient clarity on higher topics. I take the liberty therefore, for once, of writing to you in French; you will have the goodness to excuse me, and, besides, this will not in any way displease nor inconvenience you since you understand French well enough to make excellent puns: once in fact you called me a 'begue' (a "beg" in Albanian/Turkish is a nobleman, the French word is a "stammerer"), although I am rather good at talking - and another time an "ours" (bear) because I live in a street which according to an old religious legend is called Bears Street. But let's return to business.

I am certain, and I tell you in all sincerity, that you have a somewhat unusual intelligence and that your free spirit soars above the pettiness of religions and sects. But I believe that your prolonged stay in Turkey has not allowed you to keep abreast of certain things. Thus, you think without any doubt that in France they will take pity on the situation which fate has dealt us; do not deceive yourself my friend, there is no country where the hatred of liberty is so forcefully dominant as in France. This country adores despotism, and its greatest demonstrations in favour of liberty have taken a despotic form. The other countries in Europe are worse. So, what are you expecting from these people?

I wrote an article of 80 pages entitled '*An essay on the future of Albania and its attempts for independence in the 19th century. Ali Tepeleni. The revolution of 1831. The insurrection of 1866. Abdul-beg and the uprising of 1879-80; the role of Bektashism in this uprising. The contemporary movement. Apostolo Margariti and Father Faverial. Nacio and the anti-hellenic movement.'* This article took me three months. I sent it to the largest periodical in Europe. The director replied that the article was very interesting and could have an international relevance: (I showed this letter to your brother); the director added, however, that certain passages, in the very interest of the cause, needed to be deleted: I was astonished to see that he wanted me to remove everything about Bektashism, apart from a dozen or so pages; in other words, he wanted an article on an interesting question concerning religious philosophy; without reference to the claims and rights of Albania. I preferred to throw the article on the fire, for it would have increased the circulation of the journal but not profited our unhappy mountains.

For the daily press, it is even worse. One should write in newspapers such as '*La Libre Parole*', which has 600,000 readers, to make any kind of impression. All these newspapers have a passion which they pursue exclusively. However, through several friends that I have, I try to introduce here and there some words on Albania, words which in the mouth of a foreigner have a thousand times more influence than a long article from us, which one always thinks is in the service of some embassy. So, in an article which I am sending you, one of my friends advises the Turks to unite with the Albanians; in the mouth of a Frenchman this simple word will carry some influence and make the naive believe that Albania exists; well, that's wrong, Albania does not exist.

And here I come to the heart of the matter. No, Albania does not exist: Albania is you and me and some other souls fond of justice and truth; but four million indifferent people and traitors could easily oppose these fifty or so men. Could we, after that, reasonably demand reforms? And in whose name, we will be asked? Since nobody in Albania is showing discontent, everyone is pleased. So would you want the will of we fifty men to be opposed by that of four million individuals? What would we reply to that I ask? Nothing.

And what will happen inevitably is that in a quarter of a century we shall pass from the hands of the Sultan into those of the Slavs, Greeks or Italians as the vile slaves that we are. Who will defend our native soil? The members of '*Drita*' perhaps. Let us leave joking aside. Let us be friends with the Turks: for the moment it is in our interest; nobody contests it; but woe to those who only concern themselves with the present and neglect the future.

In order to shelter us from the future we must create a national party, in secret, not to displease the Turks. Thus, to create a national movement we must enlarge the question and consider it from the point of view of serious philosophy. Some sensible men have thought about the language; well, I think that there is an error here: a people who have passed centuries and centuries in the most complete indifference to its language will remain for a long time in this torpor, and it will only be in a hundred years that the Albanian will write his language.

We must, therefore, consider the Albanian question as a fragment of the large social question. We must say to the Albanians; *"Your country is one of the most fertile, and you die of starvation. You will have enough food if you show the door to the foreigners when the moment is right"*! This appeal will have immediate effects, and it will not be like a Samy Bey grammar: You have to be stupid to think that poor little books read by a dozen boys will create a national party. But if bread is promised you will see that the country will be transformed in a few years; for this we must create a secret society (like the Carbonari in Italy, the Filiki-Eteria in Greece before independence) on a firm basis and one which puts its members out of any danger.

But money is necessary. Who will provide it! Nothing will come of nothing. Romania, according to Victor Bérard, gives 12,000 francs annually to '*Drita*'. What is this sum for a party? If Romania saw its interest, if she thought that the death of Albania would leave her alone in the middle of a Slav ocean, like an island that the storm will certainly finish by drowning it, she would give at least 100,000 francs a year. Since she will not do it we have to turn to a government incapable of harming us, like England whose army, incapable of fighting in a mountainous country, would never play the same trick as on the Egyptians.

In a word, dear friend, we have to imitate our enemies; we must conspire and intrigue, or resign ourselves to die: we are obliged to make a choice. If I have not yet made myself understood, it would be best that our correspondence cease since it would become useless.

As for me, this is what has to be done. I do not know if the air that one breathes in Bucharest is different from that in Paris, but what I know is that it is impossible for me to understand how several press articles, one or two alphabet books and text books will recall to life a people which is dying, which has already one foot in the grave.

Yours sincerely,

F-D S-T-Konitza

PS You had a good idea in sending me your address for I was five times at your brother's asking him for it, and I was despairing of ever getting it from him.

As for Naoum Veqilharxhi's book, you need not worry; I only need it in a year's time and in the meantime I shall find it here perhaps. And then I simply asked you for it and not to put into practice the Latin maxim *'do ut des' 'ap gete me ape'*; Mourad beg's trifle is nothing for it was a journalist who gave me it.

AQSH F19 d.32/4 f12

[2] A word from 'The Great Old Man' 1897
Letter to Mr. Gladstone[1]

translated from the French by Peter Rennie

In the name of the Leagues for Albanian Independence, we sent a letter to Mr. Gladstone in which we summarised all the good that we think of those interesting martyrs: the Greeks. Here are several passages from this letter, which the abundance of material prevents us from giving in extenso.

I have the honour in sending you with this letter a copy of *'La Revue Albanaise'*. In doing this, I believe I am fulfilling a duty; it is necessary in fact that while great voices like yours, whose fame is universal, rise from the heart of humanity in defence of oppressed peoples it is necessary that these voices are not mistaken in their generosity, that they do not forget one people in favour of another, and that especially in thinking to plead for the oppressed they do not plead for the oppressors.

It is not a secret for any of those who know the history of modern Greece that this country owes its existence and its vitality to the Albanians alone. The Greeks reward us by 1) exciting Turkish fanaticism against us 2) setting up clerical bands of spies to disunite us 3) making European public opinion believe that we do not exist as a nationality, that we are a band of assassins and (what irony) thieves.

We do not exist as a nationality; this above all is the lie that the Greeks spread with all their might, and they attain it in quite a simple way: since 1877 Albania has been in revolt against the Turkish yoke, and this revolt is shown not by boasts in the Greek way, but by acts, such as refusal to do military service, pay taxes and to lay down arms: now the foreign press agencies and correspondents in Greece and in Turkey, subsidised by the Greeks, are compelled to report rumours of these intermittent, significant revolts, but they take care not to say that they happen in Albania; it is sometimes in *'Epirus'*, sometimes in *'Macedonia'*, sometimes in the province of *'Kosovo'* - always avoiding the word *'Albania'*, following a deceitful policy that one can so elegantly call *'the conspiracy of silence'*.

What consoles us in all this annoyance is the daily observation of the fact that those who visit the Balkans always report a profound contempt for the Greeks and much sympathy for the Albanians. But this consolation is too ideal for us not to want a more tangible consolation.

The Albanians form a considerable social group, whose individual tendencies are incompatible with those of neighbouring groups. By definition it is possible that this nation may perish, but impossible that it merge with another people. This nation will be free and will live. It will free itself from the Turks with some pain. As for those great powers who have pretentions towards Albania, they will neutralise each other. Austria will not even tolerate an Italian protectorate in Albania for this would be the complete suppression of its navy, which would find itself enclosed in a veritable lake. Italy would not permit an Austrian occupation, which would be tantamount to a blockade of its eastern shores. We only fear the Greeks because they possess a formidable army, deceit; and their deceit must be immense since they have been able to twist the sympathy of the greatest men whom the world honours.

Here is the reply which Mr.Gladstone has honoured us with:

To Mr.Trank Spirobeg, editor of Albania
London 6 April 1897

Sir,

I have the honour of acknowledging receipt of your letter of 29 March.
I do not make any distinction between the Albanians, Greeks and other people with regard to their rights to liberty, justice and humanity.
It seems to me inappropriate for you to begin your plea for the Albanians by laying severe charges against the Greeks, who are at this moment engaged in an honourable task. In the present state of my knowledge of the question I regret being unable to say any more.
I am, etc.
W Gladstone

from *'La Revue Albanaise'*
Year 1, volume 1,1897-98

[3] Brussels, 18 August 1897

translated from Albanian by Paulin Kola

To Theodor A. Ippen[2]
Austro-Hungarian Consul
Shkodër

Sir,

Having received the letter you honoured me with, I don't know how to thank you on the good wishes you express for the mission we've undertaken. Your congratulations and wishes are more invaluable coming, as they do, from yourself. The Austro-Hungarian consuls have all, to varying degrees, helped the Albanian renewal. Was it not an Austrian consul, Hahn, who worked and thought for about thirty years about the publication of the first precious monument on the Albanians?

From a literary point of view, I am of the opinion that our undertaking has a limited aim: inspiring most Albanians with the desire to support the standardisation of their language, rationally fusing the Albanian dialectal differences. We have also managed to give the language a wider spread and its vocabulary a deeper richness.

Politically, although Albania's impact remains limited by virtue of its being in the hands of the leaders of the Albanian movement, we have managed to create amongst them a lively trend against Hellenisation and against Turkish centralising designs.

Sadly, Italian propaganda, supported by the pseudo-Albanians of Calabria and Sicily, constitutes a worrying progress among nationalist circles; whilst our possibilities have not permitted us to efficiently deal with intrigues originating from that side of the Adriatic. Capitalising on the ignorance of our compatriots, the Italians truly believe that they can convince them that Albania's union with Italy would be very useful; whereas such a unification with Austria would be a disaster. However, clever Albanians are fully aware that unification with Italy would lead the former to misery and a comprehensive economic catastrophe, while, united with Hungary, it would be free to develop on all three accounts: national, economic and intellectual. This opinion, which I have had the chance to observe in many an Albanian, despite the fact that current circumstances forbid its open reaffirmation, is what I and many of my friends also share, i.e. that, were full political autonomy for us not feasible, Albania would, nonetheless, be lucky to be able to enjoy an administrative autonomy through a political and military union with the Austrian Empire.

With time, one day, it will probably be possible to show our compatriots the way to better judge events, rather than falling a prey to intrigues and pseudo-Albanians.

Please accept, Sir, the assurance of my highest consideration.
Trank Spiro Beg (Faik Bey Konitza)

from *'Faik Konitza'* by Jup Kastrati,
Gonlekaj Publishing Company, New York 1995

[4] Brussels, 26 November 1897

translated from Albanian by Paulin Kola

To Baron Goluchowski[3]
Vienna

Dear Baron,

I have the honour to present to Your Excellency through this letter a summary of the joint speech we delivered yesterday.
Like all other issues, that which concerns us should be dealt with from three aspects: I) the aims to be pursued; II) the means to achieve them; III) obstacles to be overcome.

Firstly. The aim to be pursued and achieved should be:

1) developing an Albanian national feeling perfectly aware of the fundamental differences they have with the Turks

2) rallying all forces around a unified centre to enable joint action of whatever character

3) working so that all Albanians, while within the law and respect for the governing authorities, understand which way their aspirations towards economic and intellectual progress should be channelled, were unforeseen circumstances to precipitate the dissolution of the Eastern Question.

Secondly. The means to be used:

a) The newspaper which, edited in the Tosk, Geg and French, should publish folk songs, historical chronicles, patriotic poems, economic issues, political commentaries in the shape of news, which must neither incur the distrust of the Porte through its hostile comments, nor push the Albanians, through favourable commentaries, to adopt a favourable attitude towards the Sublime Porte; the newspaper should also publish news and reports from all over Albania, so that regular and viable links can be established between all Albanian cities; letter from Serbia, Bulgaria, Greece, Bosnia; an explanation of necessary reforms; on every edition, a favourable report on all religions in Albania, so that a decisive blow is dealt to the prejudice amongst all Albanians that religion prohibits the use of their mother tongue, etc. etc.

b) The publication, two or three times a year, of simple, small leaflets in thousands of issues and in both dialects, in which the national feeling will develop though questions and answers that would bypass direct involvement in politics.

c) The foundation of an all-embracing association ('Albanian Renewal' Konitza calls it) whose members, through the power of speech would be able to accomplish what the newspaper does in print, and whose essential details have been worked out but will be unveiled to the Albanians only after they've undergone the judgement of Your Excellency.

d) Correspondence: regular and continued links should be established with all Albanians who could exercise any kind of influence in the desired sense.

e) The intermittent dispatch of a good correspondent to Serbia or wherever there are Albanians, who pass half a year in Albania, to set up branches of the association there, teach people to read, distribute leaflets and, if need be, organise meetings.

f) Schools: they should engage our liveliest interest, the more so since Albanians wholeheartedly desire their opening; however, on the one hand there's no initiative and on the other there's a shortage of teachers. It would be necessary, therefore, to send petitions to the Ottoman government from all the spots where these schools are needed. Apart from the Albanian language, which should be the basic language of the curriculum, a course in Turkish would be needed to appease the Porte, as well as courses in French and German which, being a novelty, I'm certain would gratify the Albanians. The schools would accept the management of "Albanian Renewal" (Renaissance Albanaise) founded in Albania, so that no other influence would be passed from teacher to student and from the students to their families.

g) Religions: amicable relations ought to be established among all the clergy, especially the Bektashi, whose influence, at this stage, could be useful; in the eventuality of what could come about in the future, the tendency should be fully developed towards a religious autonomy.

Thirdly: Among the obstacles to be overcome:

a) Traditional distrust on the part on the part of the Sublime Porte remains the most serious obstacle. The *'cult'* should be shed of extolling the Turkish government, because this could have an undesirable effect on the psyche of the Albanians; all criticism should be discontinued, and an almost friendly stance adopted to force it , through capable policy, to believe that it is having to deal with a peaceful, fundamentally intellectual, movement, devoid of political ambitions.

b) Hatred among Albanians stemming from their relligious differences is another obstacle; but this obstacle will disappear as we will befriend the heads of the clergy.

c) Foreign propaganda: foreign propaganda activities will be eradicated only if we, continually, decisively and passionately, unveil before the Albanians the facts that reject these intrigues, and if we unveil the consequences that could result were these intrigues left unchallenged.

d) The Albanians abroad: it would be more than useful were their moral authority over the Albanians to come to an end. We shall achieve this proving, facts and documents, that some work for Italy, some for Bulgaria or Greece, and others for their own self-interests. Consequently, we shall ingratiate the good will of the Porte, which - as I have good grounds to believe - attaches excessive importance to Bucharest's propaganda. Of additional necessity in this activity against Romanian Albanians is the fact that the press, and consequently European public opinion has slowly started to take them to represent the Albanians. This is wrong as only a few Orthodox and Catholics are able to make their voice heard, whereas the Muslims - the overwhelming majority in the country - have demonstrated that they endorse only the journal *'Albania'*. However, this media perception could prove detrimental at a crucial moment, hence the need to rectify it.

Lastly, in conclusion, let me restate that all our activities and endeavours should be permeated by these two ideas: no party should be set up, but all should rally around the same goal; the newspaper (journal), the association, the schools, propaganda - all should bear the stamp of a spontaneous movement wherein allegiances, friendships or sympathies should in no way affect our encouragement.

This, dear Baron, is on general lines the content of the talks we had yesterday. I have thought hard on all these issues, going deeper into all detail. Your Excellency will be provided with frequent updates on our activities via the Brussels Imperial and Royal Legation.

Please accept, Your Excellency, Mr Baron, the assurances of my highest consideration.

Faik Bey Konitza (Trank Spiro Beg)

from *'Faik Konitza'*, by Jup Kastrati.
Gonlekaj Publishing Company, New York 1995

[5] Brussels, 1 January 1898

translated from Albanian by Paulin Kola

To His Excellency,
Baron Goluchowski,
Minister for Foreign Affairs of Austro-Hungary,
Vienna

Mr Baron,

I have the honour to submit to Your Excellency, in conjunction with this letter, the complete and ad litteram translation of issue VIII of the *'Albania'* journal, 25 issues of which I mailed to You yesterday. The journal was printed later than I had envisaged; this was because the printing house was closed over Christmas coinciding with the final stages of its completion.

As I have had the honour to bring to the attention of Your Excellency before, editing this issue, it being transitional in regarding the new stance to be adopted vis-à-vis the Turkish government, was fraught with difficulties; I think I have overcome these. Nevertheless, should anything in issue VIII be incompatible with the views of Your Excellency, can you please, Baron, be kind enough to honour me with your advice, so that this can be avoided in future issues.

Upon my return from Vienna, I immediately wrote to my best correspondent in Istanbul requesting that he let me know his views on the likelihood of success of initiating an active propaganda in Albania to obtain the early awakening of national sentiments. The correspondent replied by sending alongside an interesting letter a list of people who would be grateful to regularly receive *'Albania'*, who, hitherto, have only managed to get hold of clips from the journal from friends in Istanbul. The list, as I noticed with surprise and happiness, contained the names of several influential pashas and beys, the Prishtina's mufti, Elbasan's chief justice and the Orthodox bishop of this city. However, my correspondent is of the opinion that it is illusory to attempt distributing the newspaper via Turkish mail, even if these newspapers were to be full of praise for the Sultan. In point of fact, the less influential people who would receive the newspaper would be detained, remaining in custody until these newspapers, mailed to Istanbul, would be translated and declared harmless; under the Turkish system, this would incur a six-month jail sentence; and we would be achieving nothing but alienating useful people from our own propaganda. Nothing of the sort would, perhaps, befall influential people; at any rate, the newspaper would be banned by the governors.

Hence, the imperative necessity of finding a clever and daring patriot, who would agree to become our newspaper man: he would go to collect a large parcel of newspapers in Durrës, and, on his way back, he would leave behind issues, wherever needed, so that, in Preveza in fifteen days' time, he would find the subsequent issue of the newspaper: he would then depart towards Durrës and so on uninterruptedly, It is not difficult to find a newspaper man as such; finding a suitable individual for our purpose remains the principal difficulty, i.e. finding someone who could speak Geg and Tosk, be able to read and write in Albanian, be capable, clever and a patriot. Having instructed all my correspondents, I hope the right man will be found.

In the meantime, I have not ignored direct involvement in the issue of schools. Something that occurred recently in Istanbul appears hopeful. The Bucharest Albanians, who, with the exception of two or three individuals, are all café-goers, have, as a joke, sent a threatening note to the sultan. Sami Bey Frashëri, manager of the Turkish daily *'Sabah'*, who occupies high office in the administration and who, alongside his brother, writes most of the Albanian books published in Istanbul, signed "N.H.F.", and the man also considered by the Turks to be the chairman of each and every national movement, has been summoned to Jilldiz Qoshk to explain the significance of that note.

He replied saying he did not know anything, he was opposite the note. However, if the Albanians demanded schools, that was to be seen as an effort to stem the spread of Slavism and Hellenism. The sultan's secretary-general responded that Albanians are entitled to demand schools in their own language, but should not do it in this manner. This appears to suggest that the Porte will not object to the opening of Albanian schools for long.

However, given that this objection could last for another three or four years, it would have to be lifted through the establishment of some schools without any permission, wherever this is possible. In this context, I have written to one of my erudite correspondents, who has expressed his readiness to return to Dibra to help create the suitable climate to open national schools, and, set up an Albanian schools upon receiving authorisation from the *'elders'* of the land. This man possesses a valuable trait: apart from being a sincere patriot, he also wears a turban, i.e. he is an imam. In a district like Dibra, where all the Albanians belong to the Muslim faith and religious passions reign supreme, only a turbaned Albanian can be assured of success. Lastly, my correspondent speaks of an elderly Tosk, a clever and capable man, and outstanding patriot of immense bravery, who also remains committed to opening national schools. I have sought to establish direct links with these two individuals, in order to be able to create an idea of what their possibilities are and whether they share our opinions on a number of issues.

More than anyone else, I'd rather believe that it would be useful to open schools without permission to think that Turkish government may, conceivably, give evidence of ill will. One of my friends, Shahin Teki Bey Kolonja[4], high school principal in Dedeagac, having been granted leave for six months, went to Istanbul to request permission to open a newspaper, half in Albanian half in Turkish *"to fight against the separatist tendencies of a number of Albanians living abroad"* (We have agreed that the principal aim of the newspaper would be to create readers in Albania, who, having learned to read and acquired a desire to read, would eventually be able to receive the *'Albania'* newspaper. Unaware of this arrangement of ours, the Porte will certainly deem useful for Turkey Shahin Teki Bey's request and almost certainly grant it. However, the public education minister kept him waiting for six months, after which he gave this explanation: *"I did not forward your request, aware that it would have been futile to do so"*.

I can lastly state that this preliminary outline of what can be done is inspiring: the future alone will be able to testify the outcome of our first endeavour.

Please accept, Your Excellency, Mr Baron, the assurances of my highest respect and loyalty.

Faik Bey Konitza

from *'Faik Konitza'* by Jup Kastrati,
Gonlekaj Publishing Company, New York 1995

[6] Brussels, 2 March 1898

translated from Albanian by Paulin Kola

To His Excellency,
Baron Goluchowski,
Minister for Foreign Affairs of Austro-Hungary,
Vienna

Mr Baron,

Let me thank Your Excellency for your kind commissioning of a report on the interesting study of Albanian linguistics and for directing that it should be sent to me. The Albanian alphabet based on the Turkish script, as proposed by the competent author of the comparative table, is comprehensive and practicable; it is very similar to the one I had envisaged, with the exception of the Spanish letter ñ, which, occurring so frequently in Albanian, would, in my opinion, have to be marked with a clearer and more likely letter, so that it could immediately alert the reader to its true significance. This is, however, not too significant an observation. Once Issue 12 has been published, I will adapt the newspaper format so that it is easier to distribute and so that it could come out twice a month with one-fourth or one-third of its current pages in Albanian, with a Turkish script.

Issues 8 & 9 of *'Albania'* have—one or two issues, some directly some indirectly—reached these cities: Delvinë, Dibër, Durrës, Korçë, Mat, Manastir, Prevezë, Sentori and some counties like Starovë, Tiranë, Zagorie. We have also sent it to about twenty other places, but some have been returned; we are not sure whether the rest have reached their destinations. I am not referring here to territory under Turkey, which is of second-hand importance, despite the fact that a large number of newspaper copies have been dispatched there too.

We have received a letter from Elbasan, via Bucharest, where, after requesting that the journal *'Albania'* be sent there, we were informed that a bey from Elbasan, Shukri Sulçebeu, who passed away a few months ago, has, in his testament, bequeathed a large house to us to use as an Albanian school building. They request that a petition be sent to the Sultan from Bucharest to request permission to open this school to be named '*Albanian School of Hamidije*', which would set an example for future schools in Albania. It would, perhaps, be simpler and better for them to petition the Sultan themselves from Elbasan; they, nonetheless, think that a petition sent from a big European city would have a better chance of success. I am of the opinion that any such intervention is doomed to failure; for it is apparent that the Sultan harbours a strong hatred and mistrust for the Albanians and will resist any of their demands.

Nonetheless, I have written to Tahir Pasha, chief of the Albanian royal guard. He comes from Northern Albania, has a daily audience with the Sultan, enjoying his boundless trust. Implementing for the first time in practice Your Excellency's idea, I wrote to him in Geg with a Turkish script, saying it would be in the best interest of His Excellency, the Sultan, to authorise the opening of Albanian schools, because that would facilitate the disarmament of the population, etc. etc. He will, maybe, put in a good word to his boss, urged by his conscience if not his wit.

However, aware of the possibility that these endeavours could lead to nothing, I have kept an open mind on the establishment of schools in Dibër and other districts like Dibër, as advised by one of my Istanbul correspondents. Unfortunately, as Your Excellency is well aware, the Albanians have but a vague idea of what is entailed by regular correspondence and systematic and speedy work; they are keen to read letters and other publications and to benefit from them, but find no need to make haste. I have exchanged four letters with one of our Geg professors, but have been unable, so far, to tackle every issue. Therefore, I will only inform Your Excellency on schools when I shall be in a position to have some concrete results.

In lieu of the call, which the people of Manastir were to distribute, I have drafted another one, the French translation of which I have the honour to enclose for Your Excellency. I think it contains nothing that would prompt action on the part of the Turkish government. Were Your Excellency to accept it unchanged, I would print it in a thousand copies, in Turkish and Albanian, using Turkish script. As I understand it, to be able to awaken Albanian national sentiments, a copy would better be sent to every city or district where there is even a single Albanian who can read. We would attain our goal if we were to sent thirty a week, in sealed envelopes.

Please accept, Your Excellency, Mr Baron, the assurances of my highest respect and loyalty.

Faik Bey Konitza

from *'Faik Konitza'*, by Jup Kastrati,
Gonlekaj Publishing Company, New York 1995

[7] Brussels, 21 November 1897

translated from Albanian by Paulin Kola

To Visarion Dodani [5]

Dear brother Dodani,

I was glad to read your beautiful letter. You asked why I didn't write for so long? The reason that I have been deeply concerned. I truly believe now that foreigners are right: Albanians cannot secure their own freedom.

Wretched slaves for more than five-hundred years, slaves they will die. Let me say it openly: I have no expectations that anything at all will happen, and I'm sure all those who do a bit of thinking, share this opinion of mine. To have had expectations, Albanians would have had to have established sound committees in thousands of places, agitators to go to every village in Albania, dailies and other newspapers across Europe. They have nothing!

Five hundred years of slavery has not shifted them. The well-off did not help, the poor do not work. What can we expect, then? On the letters, you are right, but I have been able to publish the newspaper with the assistance of the Istanbul fellows; what will I do once I have enraged them too? Therefore, the issue of the letters will rest for a bit, before we can open a *'discussion'*.

I embrace you and remain your brother.

Faik Bey Konitza

from *'Faik Konitza'* by Jup Kastrati,
Gonlekaj Publishing Company, New York 1995

[8] Brussels, 11 June 1898

translated from Albanian by Paulin Kola

To Visarion Dodani,

My dear brother, Visarion Dodani,

Your Excellency's letter pleased me immensely, being, as it is, devoid of hypocrisy. I therefore want to openly say a couple of words.

It is true that were *'Shqipëria'* and *'Albania'* to agree, the rest would be too easy. If this is the case, why, then, did they not agree? With a lot of heartache I can say that this is why: today, we received five or six letters from some compatriots teaching us something very important.

Pandeli Evangjeli appears to be being paid by the Greeks to stem the development of an Albanian national sentiment. Consequently, the compatriots say, this 'sir' does nothing to promote Albanian, nor does he bother that the Korça school improve and neither does he speedily publish the Bibles we send, but keeps them concealed for months and years on end; in sum, *'Dituria'* looks like being a trap wherein our genuine compatriots end up working less and less in coldness and slumber. It's not worth mentioning that we've lent no credence to these wicked actions, for, had we done so, we'd have exposed them.

The compatriots who wrote also pointed out: Mr Pandeli is working day and night to alienate the daily *'Shqipëria'* from the Albanians that it daily deals with.

Like a brother let me repeat: we've never believed these things. Nevertheless, cold had now set in between us…

Regarding the Sultan, L. and yourself are both right, he's a clever, wise and civilised monarch; praising him, we hope to wheedle him into allowing our schools. His highness, the Sultan's chief secretary, Mr Tahsim Bey, has written on behalf of the King to invite us to go to Istanbul to publish *'Albania'*, given that there are twenty-thousand Albanians there, and the government is to assist us with the distribution of the paper; however, my health at this moment does not permit me and Viska to go to Istanbul, so let's wait and see.

Strongly wishing that cold may never settle between us two, I warmly embrace you and so does Viskë Babatasi.

Your brother,

F. Konitza

from *'Faik Konitza'* by Jup Kastrati,
Gonlekaj Publishing Company, New York 1995

[9] Brussels, 16 June 1898

translated from Albanian by Paulin Kola

To Visarion Dodani

My dear brother Dodani,

Don't think I'm cross. How can one become cross when one sees a true brother speak from the depth of his heart. There's only one thing that makes me cross and wounds my soul: some compatriots who are unable to criticise me openly, working in a wicked way behind my back, in places where I'm not and am therefore unable to undo the slander ...

'Shqipëria' is improving by the day; believe it or not, think that I'm flattering you, if you wish, but the fact remains that ever since Meksi packed it in, the daily has gone up in circulation and in quality.

I can easily subscribe to what you write, given that it's what I think as well. Let me add, however: there are hundreds of thousands of fanatical Albanians. What can we do; we need a daily that would be acceptable to these people! Therefore *'Albania's'* form is slightly different from *'Shqipëria's'* .

I enclose an article, extracted from the large German daily *'Frankfurter-Zeitung'* of 5 July, which, as you are well aware, is very influential in Europe. Speaking on Albania's autonomy, it states that *'Albania'* and the Albanians of Bucharest are working hard to this end. Given its harsh tone, and the fact that it enters into polemics with me, I can't publish it in *'Albania'*. However, you can translate and publish it if you like given that it's very significant. I implore you to send us your picture, which we'll need in three or four months.

I embrace you as a brother,

Faik Konitza

from Faik Konitza by Jup Kastrati,
Gonlekaj Publishing Company, New York 1995

[10] Brussels, 4 August 1898

translated from Albanian by Paulin Kola

To Visarion Dodani

Dear brother,

Let me respond to those few words in the postcard you recently honoured me with.

You've spoken once before on the self-styled 'Italian- Albanians'. To be frank with you, I haven't published anything else against them; but now that they're fighting us, we're responding. We'll boldly and readily engage in the confrontation; readily because we're Albanians who never tire of things; boldly because justice is on our side. You have received issue No. 4 of *'Albania'*, in which you will have seen how we've laid bare Anselmo's lies. It's all very clear: anyone capable of judgement will see that we are right. Tell me, dear brother, if, by speaking ill of Anselmo, we offend some compatriots. I think these patriots of ours are unaware of their deeds, for, were it to be otherwise, we would be justified in spitting into the faces of these people, who would no longer be patriots but traitors.

Eh, dear brother! Can't you see that our two papers have a huge task to fulfil before History: in order to be able to do this, they ought to co-operate closely; as you say, we share the same view; why should we be divided by the bickering of those ... from Italy?

So far in Europe, there have been lots of good things said about the Albanians. These were undone in a flash by a certain Italian called Baldacci, who wrote that the Albanians are wild and beastly. Do you know how Anselmo describes this enemy of ours? "Il nostro illustro amico Baldacci" Anselmo, has therefore written that the most contemptible enemy of the Albanian nation is his best friend!...

So, brother, pull yourself together and don't be taken in by the bickering of those who speak well of Anselmo. However, do as you please. But let me openly say that I deplore seeing a patriot like yourself defending the so-called Albanians of Italy. We could somehow afford to be friends with people like Schiroj, but not an Anselmo who I'm going to fight until he stops lying and believes that the Albanians of *'Albania'*, those from Shkodër, Mirditë and all of Albania are not for sale.

Hoping that one day you'll understand how mad you are, I warmly shake your hand.

Faik Konitza.

from *'Faik Konitza'* by Jup Kastrati,
Gonlekaj Publishing Company, New York 1995

[11] Brussels, 3 April 1900

translated from Albanian by Paulin Kola

To Visarion Dodani

Honourable patriot Dodani,

I wholeheartedly thank you for the letter you honoured me with. I have always held you in great esteem, something I proved before the world by praising your good deeds. But I did not mail *'Albania'* to you, or the other man in Bucharest, and neither did I communicate with anyone else there for this reason:

I came to Bucharest two years ago to meet you. An aide to the Sultan, called Murat Toptani[6], was travelling with me. The Bucharest Albanians, who are rich and pretend to be patriots, wasted about 10 000 francs on the Sultan's servant, who, afterwards … (excuse my expression) left for Istanbul; while, for an albeit distant relation of Ali Pasha, someone who spent years in Europe longing for Albania, who first began the struggle and continues working and suffering for five years running, no one thought it appropriate to help me, not for my own sake but for Boçari's dictionary, which I wanted to publish alongside some other books.

I did, therefore, measure and experience the patriotism of the Bucharest Albanians, at first hand, and came to the conclusion that the honourable thing to do would be to wash my hands of them.

But let me repeat that I have never ceased to praise you, as proved by what I wrote in *'Albania'*.

With longing,

Faik Konitza

from *'Faik Konitza'* by Jup Kastrati,
Gonlekaj Publishing Company, New York 1995

[12] Brussels, 29 November 1901

translated from Albanian by Paulin Kola

To Visarion Dodani

Dear brother Dodani,

You gave me immense pleasure with those letters you honoured me with. But why so rarely? Why like the sun that rises once a year? On your request to know about Prince Aladro, I can reassure you that he is a honourable man whose intentions appear laudable and praiseworthy. You'd better write to him too. You could congratulate him on the setting up of the Skanderbeg Prize, which, this year, he awarded to one of my Geg colleagues who's printed some books. Prince Aladro has also contributed thousand of francs for a geographical map of Albania, which will be published by the end of the Calendar. He's ready to spend more, but I fear he could get skinned by some shameless bastards.

I do not know what to say on that man from Kolonja you ask about, Shahin, for I don't know him. Let's wait. Time only will tell what kind of person he is. I was greatly disturbed to read that the great dictionary of our great Kritoforidhi has fallen into Greek hands. Can you please, dear brother, send me an article on how this came about? I'll publish it in the front page of issue 1 of the year VI. Should you be reluctant to use your own name, send me a letter, and I'll write an article thence. I'll be glad to send you the missing issues of *'Albania'*; but today I'm packing up my books and other papers as I have to move house. Once this is over, I'll satisfy your desire.

Thank you for Zyko Kamberi's[7] poems. They are beautiful, but I do not want to alienate Albanian women…

The '*Bashkimi Association*' in Shkodër has published six books which I'll soon send to you; its hot-headed and strong members will do many things: some that I've known have shown this. I left *'Albania's'* ABC for a couple of years, siding with them. It's better for all wise patriots to do the same as it's a shame before the civilised world that we use a dirty and uncouth ABC like the one produced by the Sultan's lickspittles.

Best regards to friends and patriots. I embrace you.

Faik Konitza

The address of the Prince of Aladro:
S.A. Don Juan, marquis de Aladro, Prince de Kastriot
9 Square Lamartine, Paris

from *'Faik Konitza'* by Jup Kastrati,
Gonlekaj Publishing Company, New York 1995

[13] Brussels, April-May 1902

translated from Albanian by Paulin Kola

Open letter to Shahin Bey Kolonja, Manager of '*Drita*'[8]

Sir,

I read the open letter you wrote in '*Drita*. Your slanders make me happy, because they relieve me of a burden. It would have been a dirty job to praise someone and subsequently attack him. So I thank you that, by starting this, you relieve me and force me to speak openly. This is not the language you used when Ismail Bey Vlora sacked you in Brussels.. Do you remember? But this is typical of the ungrateful: when weak, they obey; when they recover somewhat, they vilify…

You state that Konica is populated with Greeks and that I must be one of them. I would have been honoured to have been Greek, first because people are proud of their nationality, secondly because the Greeks may be hostile to Albania but not to themselves and thirdly because the Greeks have enlightened the world. However, there's no household in the whole of Albania that is more Albanian than mine.

A French writer, referring to my great grandfather, Zejnel Bey Konica, whose daughter was the mother of Ali Pashë Tepelena, wrote: *"This Konica Bey is a powerful Albanian bey, linked by blood with the first Albanian households of Toskëri, and the marriage of whose daughter, Hanko, to Veli Bey Tepelena, strengthened him, contributing to the greatness of Ali Pasha"*. Aravantini has said: *"Zejnel Bey of Konitsa, an Albanian Bey of the most powerful of his time, whose great grandfather was a pasha, married his daughter…"*

From these books, and many more, it is clear that my family have been known as Albanians since the sixteenth century. Of you, Sir, I require not 400 but 150 years of Albanianhood. Are you Albanian? Could you have been vomited into Albania from some Anadolli quarters, attested by the family links you've established with Anadollaks? I have always believed you to be Albanian; but since you have the cheek to think me Greek, could it be that in so doing you are trying to conceal your true nationality?

You wouldn't have written that had you had a brain. If there were many Greeks in Konica; if Frashëri were a region populated by Vlahs to the extent that Romanians have turned it into the hub of their propaganda, establishing a Vlah school into the bargain; - the Albanians of these areas are all the more to be praised for, preserving your nationality in the midst of Albania is no big deal, whereas it's hard work if you are surrounded with foreigners. My house is the only one in Konica to speak Albanian, and has been doing so for hundreds of years - and today, a peasant rascal dares say that I am not Albanian!!

I referred to Ali Pashë Tepelena. This reminds me of something else. I have heard, or been told by yourself in a moment of honesty which I valued, that your grandfather worked as a servant of Ali Pasha's. If he's been a *'servant'* of a household so closely linked to mine, I think I see here the same wicked envy against myself that servants often harbour against their bosses. Or is it not so? You say that I have vulgarised my vocabulary. What other words can one possibly use against someone as vulgar as you? You interpret mature speech to be a sign of fear; you are incapable of appreciating irony and fine jokes. What else is left? If you prefer fine words, wash your hair first to get rid of the lice, dip your feet twice a day in phenic acid so they won't stink - then let us see.

You say you're writing to me for the last time. I'm also doing this for the last time, given that you're not worth me referring to you again, these remarks being sufficient. But I won't do the same about the paper appearing under your name: I will unfailingly attack it, until all the world is made aware of your intentions.

Faik Konitza

from *'Faik Konitza'* by Jup Kastrati.
Gonlekaj Publishing Company, New York 1995

[15] Where? When?,

To the Albanians

translated from Albanian by Paulin Kola

To date, I have not spoken of myself, as we need to cultivate the language and awaken our people, not show off. However, now that some shameless people have begun slandering or are of the opinion that they're offending me, let me say a couple of words. Only a couple, which will be Shahin's words.

Perhaps some might be ashamed to admit what I'm proud of: please understand that the six years that I've had *'Albania'* have been six years of difficulties to make ends meet. The very many Albanians who've been to Brussels and met me know that I have never been able to overcome these difficulties. All the assistance I have received or which I will receive - which I will never forget, not being ungrateful - has gone to the benefit of national propaganda; to those many people who offered their wallets to me I have suggested who they should help, where they should spend the money, but never have I asked for anything for myself; I have neglected many offers of work which I could have gained had I left *'Albania'*.

Consequently, I have always lived in dire straits. In December 1901, someone who'd lived with me for about a year wrote me a letter in which, among others, stated: *"I only know how much you suffer for 'Albania' … Food or no food …"* The person writing these lines was no one else but Shahin Bey Kolonja.

This rascal is probably not wise enough to appreciate the great psychological changes underwent by the Albanian nation since *'Albania'* first appeared, but he knows well that there's been nothing in it for me, he's aware of my difficulties, has written on them, has told others of them; he knows that for as along as I'll stick to it I'll be lost and broke, and were I to resign - even through no misdeed - I would be saved; he is aware that I have always had the will to sustain this light I lit for as long as necessary;

he knows that I have never been weak, nor will I ever desist. He knows that I don't complain, I don't tire, that I am happy to be as I am.

Despite all this, he speaks ill of me. Despite all this, he feigns ignorance. Despite all this, he humiliates me for my service to the nation, for Istanbul's worthless minions, those who take bribes and work for the Turkish language have never sacrificed anything for Albania.

Do I have to add more? Would Shahin's words not be enough to open everyone's eyes? Is this not self-punishment? Is it not crystal-clear that if rascals speak ill of me this is because I have laid bare their lies, I've had the gumption to expose them and to stop them playing with Albanians?

Were a government change to occur in Turkey, all these patriots, who have become Albanians seeing Turkey's end near, will again turn Turk, for Turkicised is their soul. Were something to be done with Albania, those who've been the last to serve their nation will be the first to *'rake in'* benefits.

These individuals, of feeble minds, devoid of programme, motivated by nothing but lies and a desire to position themselves to benefit from what tomorrow could bring, these are Albania's shame and its wound. These people I will attack, we will tirelessly attack.

Faik Konitza

from *'Faik Konitza'* by Jup Kastrati,
Gonlekaj Publishing Company, New York 1995

[15] London, on the 9th of November 1908

translated from Albanian by Paulin Kola

Letter to Mr. Kristo D. Qiriasi
For the '*Bashkimi Club*' in Monastir
'*Albania*' 1896

Dear Patriot

Three days ago I received your letter of Autumn II, 29. '*inviting*' me to the self-styled '*congress*' only a week before it convenes, you think I am a '*Prince*' Albert Gjikë who's made it a habit whenever he invites friends to dinner, to mail the invitation five minutes before the time dinner is to be set. It goes without saying that, owing to hundreds of known reasons, I will not attend the 'congress'; on the other hand, you can't say you didn't invite me. You say you sent another "*invitation twenty days ago*" (i.e., according to your letter, on 10 Autumn II); this untruth is too vulgar to deserve a mention; the English mail service has never mislaid any of my letters in over seven or eight years. However, had you even sent the first '*invitation*', could I ask why the call was sent to the Greek newspapers two months before it reached the oldest Albanian journal?

Rest assured that a Congress on the ABC will be convened. But it will be '*the right Congress, by the right men, in the right time, at the right place*'. Translate this to the Turkish pilaff-cooks and to the Christian lickspittles you have hastily gathered in Macedonia.

There's one thing I like about your self-styled '*congress*' : its poetic aspects. Most of you are shepherds and whenever I think of you, I seem to feel the refreshing caress of the breeze of Theocritus' idylls.
"Arhjete bokolikas, mosai filasi, arhjet' aoidas"
"Ady men a mos-hos gargetai, ady de hja Bos,
Ady de hja syrigks, hjo bokolos…"

Something bothers me. In an effort to give vent to your poetic inspiration, you chose not the music but the script. For if Thyrsis and Daphne and the others of Theocritus' shepherds played the flute so soothingly and sang so beautifully, - can Hasani and Belluli, Risto and Jorgaqi, and the other shepherds of this *'congress'* write? I regret to tell you that I have my doubts.Permit me, holy patriot, to cite from your letter.

You write: *"mbajet", "pe"*. This form can only be used in discredited low language, sermo proletarius; the educated would say *"mbahet", "prej"*. Again you write: *"vëjuerë", "dëgjonetë", "të parëtë"*. Are you mad? Ninety five words in a hundred are paroxitone in Albanian; shepherds like you, keen on lengthening the end of each word with an *ë*, a letter which, in Tosk, has the value of a full syllable, manage to turn ninety-five words in a hundred into proparoxitone, transforming therefore completely the character and nature of the language. I suggest you clean your ears from the Turkish pudding to be able to hear better: you'll then notice that people outside pigsties actually say *"dëgjonet", "të parët"*, etc.

Elsewhere you write: *"dit", "an", "jasht"*. No! These words in Tosk comprise two syllables: *"ditë"*, etc. Clean your ears, clean them well. Yet in another part you use u instead of ju. You say *"u" shkruam* (you). No! *ju shkruam juve, u shkruam atyreve.* Elsewhere: *"dotu"* in a single word. No! there are three separate words here, *"do t'u"*.

Lastly, sometimes you refer to me as *"ti"* sometimes as *"ju"* (or *"u"*): *"T(dërgojmë"* and (j) *"u bëjmë"*. No, no! it's either *"ti"* throughout the letter or *"ju"*. Anyone with a command of the language does not use both at the same time, as his pen fancies it.

"Ligete bokolikas, mosai, ite, liget' aoidas". I'm sorry I learned too late that some of my friends were going to attend the *"congress"*; I know they won't take these personally. If they went, I'm sure they did this with the best of intentions.

Faik Bey Konitza

from *'Faik Konitza'* by Jup Kastrati,
Gonlekaj Publishing Company, New York 1995

[16] Boston,

translated from Albanian by Paulin Kola

To Kristo Floqi[10]

Dear Mr Floqi,

I received your letter this afternoon and I thank you for the praise of friendship and honour you bestow on me. Unfortunately, I have made arrangements for Sunday, having been unaware of a scheduled meeting this Sunday (despite the fact that the date of the meeting had been announced in four issues of *'Djelli'* which Mr Konitza received regularly), and of the fact that you'd invite me today.

I appreciate your ideas on the unification. Undoubtedly, that should be affected provided we find the right formula to do it without undoing the work we've done so far with great difficulty. Here, we have our own committee, *'Flamuri i Krujës'*, and we see no reason why we should disband it. It's natural that enterprises devoid of programme and system should be stopped, but not what has been set up with a great deal of care.

I hope you'll weigh these properly and justify me.

Yours sincerely,

Faik Konitza

from *'Faik Konitza'* by Jup Kastrati,
Gonlekaj Publishing Company, New York 1995

[17] London ,23 July 1904

translated from French by Peter Rennie

To Theodore A. Ippen

Dear Sir,

'Albania' has stopped appearing. Eight years ago when I began publication I had the honour of writing to you. During these eight years you were willing sometimes to show an interest in editing it. It is therefore natural that I send you, at the same time in expressing my gratitude, some words in the form of a conclusion. For every well-composed book, like every well-conducted business, has a prologue, intermediary chapters, and an epilogue. It is the epilogue which I offer you here.

Eight years ago my opinion was, and still continues to be, that Albania finds itself in a situation too special to be able to develop without external support. Just as the history of small western countries endlessly shows us some personalities *'embracing the party of Spain'* or *'the party of France'*, etc, to safeguard the existence of their peoples, so I was convinced that Albania ought to *'embrace a party'* and, for many reasons, the best seemed to me to be that of Austria.

As you know, I asked and obtained from your government a small grant which allowed me to pursue with a certain success these four aims: 1) to develop the culture of the Albanian language; 2) to create an atmosphere favourable to Austrian influence in giving the Albanian people the impression that it is supported by Austria; 3) to create abroad the opinion that the Albanians are favourable to Austria (and this opinion curiously enough I have managed to impose even on the Italians!); 4) to annihilate all Italo-Albanian influence or any other harmful to the tendency I want to create. This fourth point has been fully realised: I, and nobody else, uprooted the newly started influence of the Italo-Albanians which was going to be a formidable weapon in the hands of Italy.

I spared no effort to achieve these results. Convinced of the necessity for Albanians to unite in a common feeling with regard to Austria, I endeavoured to make everyone understand the need to abandon all duplicity and falsehood, to inspire by our sincerity even to Austria the desire to be useful to our cause. To be the first to give an example, I have never had two opinions: one for the newspaper, the other for private life. I have never suffered anyone to attack your policies even in private conversations; and this is the story of all my quarrels. I broke off relations with all my compatriots as well as with Aladro because I saw in them tendencies hostile to the Austrian influence; and I do not hold at all with playing a double game. By this persistent sincerity I made more impression than by my writings.

Unfortunately these efforts have been badly appreciated by your government. Sometimes it seemed to think that I was enchanted by its financial support, which is ridiculous, in view of the sum put at my disposal. Sometimes, it replied to my actions by wounding and unjustified remarks. Moreover, Vienna had an incomplete understanding of the situation in Albania.

Four years ago, your government asked me to go to Vienna to express my views on the Albanian movement: I went there - and they suggested that I try to introduce *'Albania'*, via Egypt, hiding the parcels in boxes of other merchandise: what I found amusing was not the idea of this revolutionary contraband, for it is good to try anything to overcome difficulties, but my great astonishment in seeing that they knew so little about Albania to think that it was possible to carry out attempts so complicated: so I kept the plan, which I had brought, in my pocket, since it was useless to show it. Another profound error in Vienna was to believe that there were *'influential men'*; now, you know that there are no longer such men; in High Albania perhaps, but in central and southern Albania nothing of the sort has existed for thirty or so years.

Those who think they are *'influential'* are only jokers and rascals who speculate on the ignorance which is generally found where everyone touches upon the Albanian psychology. The people are too demoralised to have any attachment, they have seen and see every day too many downfalls to believe in the importance of anyone. Look at Hassan Bey Vrioni and his son Nuzet: your government thought them influential, and yet when they went into prison and only came out dead, not one Albanian lifted a finger to help them. The only influence possible today is that which you acquire for yourself, asserting your own value.

Besides, influential men, if there were any, would be of no use since every Albanian's principle being what one can call Italophile, but not Austrophile, is that if you succeed in creating unconvinced supporters they will keep what they think to themselves; you would be lucky if they don't attack you in an underhand way to make you believe that they owe you nothing. What needs to be done is to create a tide on which everyone is drawn in spite of himself. All political movements have been organised in this way: an atmosphere must be created without trying to enrol individuals one by one, which will take a thousand years. This is my idea at least. I have never understood the importance of having many readers, but I appreciate good readers in small numbers perhaps, but intelligent and able to understand and to spread what they have understood.

To bring this plan to a successful conclusion, and quickly, you have to devise other means than those which I have at my disposal: in Vienna they do not seem to have a very clear idea of what is a people without schools, without moral support, given over to every passion and suggestion, and which is attempting to organise for the first time. Place the Bulgarians in the same conditions of isolation as the Albanians, and you will see a little that they are on the whole inferior to us.

In spite of these difficulties, I was not at all discouraged, and more than ever carried on the work I had begun. Unfortunately, a year ago, the Albanians began to be a little too badly treated; official and semi-official newspapers in Vienna spared them no attack; and your diplomacy suddenly showed itself as the protector of the Bulgarian aggressors against the Albanians, defending the little freedom and country which remains to them. In these conditions I felt uneasy and could not prevent myself from speaking out. Indeed I found myself in an unpleasant situation; on all sides I was accused of having lied in representing Austria as a friend of Albania. In the meantime I received a threatening letter from Vienna (always this unfortunate annual subvention of 100,000 francs which they harshly threatened would be withdrawn) in which I was treated as a liar and the Albanians as *'Arnauts'* (a word which the Serbs use in hatred). Naturally, I replied as I should. I had a profound respect for the person with whom I was in correspondence, but I could not do less than reply that I was not a man to be flattened. In reply, I received a very friendly word where I was assured that there had been a misunderstanding and that I should continue.

Since that time, I was encouraged to do my best, as far as the new circumstances could allow me without discrediting myself in the eyes of my compatriots. To crown it all, being neurasthenic, several months ago I was seized by one of those attacks which makes all work painful even if one persists in wanting to work. My depression was so profound that, being unable to finish an article which a Parisian review had requested almost a year ago, I had to resort to narcotic substances in order to give myself artificial strength to write and to fulfill my obligation.

In this state of health, I learn that your government, without any warning, withdraws the support on which I have counted until the last minute. It could not do this at the end of last year; it should have let me negotiate with the printer with whom I had renewed a contract and the booksellers who, for the most part, have paid their subscriptions. I confess that I am quite unable to understand why I have been put into this embarrassing position: it would have been so easy to inform me in a friendly fashion that they were no longer disposed to help me. Warned in time, I could have taken measures, and your government would have had nothing to lose.

Can it have been offended by some conciliatory words I wrote for Italy? You know well that I am neither foolish nor impudent enough to ask for financial help from a country whose queen I have many times shown in disobliging colours, and not only in *"Albania'*, but in ten other foreign journals. Only, the Italian government rendered a service to a relative of mine; it released several Albanians from prison; and I had to adopt a friendly deferential tone in this regard, drawing attention to the clique of Garibaldi and of Anselmo Lorecchio.

Frankly, with your government, one does not know what attitude to adopt. In Albania, when an unfortunate person dares to approach an imperial and royal consul, he is thrown into prison, and nothing is done to help him: for example, Mourad Bey Toptani, Hassan Bey Vrioni and his son, etc. The Vrionis died in prison because they had the reputation of being Austrophile, and you did nothing to save them when there was time. Abroad, if someone is naive enough to be sincere with you, you abandon him without warning, after years of effort on his part.

Allow me to be frank to the end, since I am writing to you for the last time. Your government pretends to want to help the Albanians get out of their miserable situation. This is all very well in theory. But in fact, what is there? Diplomatically, you have done nothing to bring about the least amount of freedom to the Albanian people. Financially even less; for your aid to the clergy or to individuals, without national intention, has no concern for the country; and I know enough about Albanian affairs to state that if you take into account those who contribute strictly to the Albanian awakening (i.e.newspapers, books, teachers), the year when you disposed of the greatest amount did not reach 20,000 francs. When one thinks that a small state like Romania set aside for one whole year 600,000 francs in its budget to help the scholarly and literary movement of the Vlachs, the figure of 20,000 from a big power for a similar aim in Albania looks like a trompe l'oeil. The moral: do not rely on diplomacy; do not rely on the cash box. However much you restrict yourself by spending methodically you spend a little; but you help to build here, you help to destroy there what you have built. Witness the *'Bashkimi'* society and the plotters who rose against it. So that 100-100 = 0.

But to return to my business, they have perhaps been very clever. But too much cleverness can harm. A state, if it wants to have a policy, ought not only to aim at cleverness. It ought also to aim for esteem and world confidence. *'I give you so much, you give me this; when I stop, you will stop.'* This is what is very good in commerce. But when someone has tried to be useful to you for seven years, you have a certain moral obligation not to abandon him in the middle of work which he was pursuing confidently; as things are, a notice is in order.

If I had acted as cavalier every time someone proposed that I adopt a line of conduct unfavourable to Austria, you would have heard about it. But I believed myself morally obliged towards your government.

After having fought so much to create in Albania a movement which ought to be more favourable to you than to ourselves, your government, forgetful or badly informed, tricks me into a cruel embarrassment. I am too much a pessimist to have ever hoped for some personal advantage. But I would never have thought of behaviour so ungentlemanly. However, I have no animosity at all. If I had any, it would have been calmed by the idea that I am unique in my kind in Albania and that those who did not appreciate me would know it one day by comparison.

I beg you to excuse the unusual length of this letter, strictly personal, and to excuse also my frankness. You are one of those who have contributed most to restoring some life to the Albanian language; all Albanians (rare unanimity) are pleased to recognise it - as well as me.

Believe, dear sir, in the sincerity of my best regards,

Faik Konitza

AQSH f.13, d3, page 8

[18] January 5, 1907

translated from Albanian by Robert Elsie

To Lef Nosi[11]

Dear Patriot,

I have been ill and away from London for several weeks and unfortunately received your letter with some delay. I was quite astounded at what you told me. Do not be surprised that I had not found out earlier. As I say, I have not been well and have only rarely been to the office. I only opened one or two letters and left them for when I was feeling better.

The infrequency of the publication of *'Albania'*, which has only appeared four times a year, is ample proof of the fact that I am not swimming in money. Otherwise, believe me, I would have helped you immediately without hesitation.

How did things go with Aladro? You would be well advised to find a back issue of the Milan newspaper *'Corriere della Sera'* in which a lead article was published five years ago strongly criticizing Aladro. *'Corriere della Sera'* is Italy's leading newspaper and it is surprising that Aladro did not react to it. The article would be of great assistance to you.

Yours,

Faik Konitza

AQSH f.44, d.21, f.113

[19] February 3, 1907

translated from Albanian by Robert Elsie

To the Chairman of the *'Bashkimi (Unity) Society'*

'AlbaniA'
A monthly Albanian Review of Literature and Politics,
Established 1896, Brussels.
London Office: 3, Oakley Crescent, City Rd., E.C.

Chairman
Bashkimi (Unity) Society
Bucharest

Dear Sir,

It was with great interest that I read the letter you sent me, in which you informed me of the amalgamation of the three national societies, *'Drita' (Light), 'Dituria' (Knowledge) and 'Shpresa' (Hope),* into one. The Albanians of Romania, ardent patriots as always, have thus given proof once again of their sentiments. I was very pleased and will make this news public by means of Albania, I have no doubt whatsoever that my readers will feel every bit as much pleasure as I do.

I would simply wish to draw your attention to a mistake which I believe the society has made. I am referring to the adoption of the name Bashkimi (Unity). As you know, a society with this name was founded in Shkodra several years ago under the aegis of the esteemed Abbot of Mirdita. It achieved quite a bit and is well known everywhere. Do you not think it would have been better to baptize your society with another name, for instance Lidhja (League) or at least Bashkimi i Ri (New Unity)? From the point of view of language, you are of course perfectly free to keep Bashkimi, but the prerogative of courtesy, which I am sure you respect all the more, causes us to pay attention to these small details. If there were two different national societies, both bearing the same name, they would often be confused with one another, and I am sure this is a problem you will not want to be faced with.

It is not my place to advise you. I am simply pointing something out to you, asking you to judge for yourself in a just manner, and to take a decision accordingly, if you so wish.

I remain,

Yours faithfully,

Faik Konitza

AQSH. f.44. d.21.page 121-123

[20] London, May 29, 1907

translated from Albanian by Robert Elsie

To Nikolla Bey Ivanaj

Albania

Dear Patriot,

I would be in anguish if I believed you thought me indifferent to your tribulations. On the contrary! Let me say here, as I will say in Albania, that I am in total sympathy with you. But I am convinced that on an occasion such as this one, more is needed than words of comfort. Genuine assistance is what is called for, which I am alas unable to provide you with at the moment. Nothing can be done through the newspapers here because your problem is much too local for the English reader. If the Cour d'Appel gives you enough time to pay, it would be a good idea to publish an appeal in Shpresa to collect money for the fine.

Cordially,

Faik Konitza

P.S. Do not regard me as indifferent. I have suffered much over the past years and for two years now, I have not written any letters or done anything for anyone.

AQSH. f.44. d.21.page 121-123

[21] London, October 24, 1907

translated from Albanian by Robert Elsie

To Nikolla Bey Ivanaj

Albania

Dear Patriot,

What I wrote in *'Albania'* is not only a sign of my friendship for you but is also the fulfilment of an obligation. Publishers of Albanian-language newspapers, at least the good ones, should support one another (there is nothing but detriment to be expected from Lidhja).

I was not able to put into practice the thought I articulated in my last letter, to which you had the kindness to reply in length from Dubrovnik, for the publication of an appeal for you, because the indifference of the Albanians is such that none of them would have responded and their silence would have been but another attack against you. They do not understand, nor do they seek ties. They do not realize that in an event such as this one which has happened to you, every kind-hearted person should be with you and protest against the shameless behaviour of a person such as Aladro. What has happened to you is a good occasion to teach Aladro a lesson. But once again, where are our men of courage?

I believe you are mistaken when you say that Mr Sotir Peci is a friend of Aladro. As to Shahin, everyone knows he is being supported by the government of Vienna. For this reason he is not, nor can he be a supporter of Aladro.

Aladro only has the support of five or six priests from Shkodra, including Mr Luigj Gurakuqi who, though an *'ardent friend'* of mine, has in secret maintained friendly relations with Aladro for the last five years. They now say that he is going to *'kiss Babatasi's foot'* because he has abandoned the *'king'* and gone off to America.

Thank you for inquiring in your last letter as to my health. I am very strong and well in all respects except for my heart which is unfortunately not in a good state. I often have an attack and my heart rages for two or three days when I feel bad and am unable to work.

A few weeks ago, a number of Albanians from Albania were here on their way to America.

Yours,

Faik Konitza

AQSH. f.44. d.21.page 121-123

[22] February 1, 1908

translated from Albanian by Robert Elsie

To Nikolla Bey Ivanaj

3, Oakley Crescent, City Rd, E.C. London,

Dear Patriot,

I was saddened to learn that the high court judge of Vienna ruled in favour of the judgment of Dubrovnik. You will therefore have to pay 100 crowns, not to mention the costs of a lawyer and transportation. Yesterday, I sent you one English pound as a small token of my sympathy. A supporter of Albania in America sent me 5 dollars, and I have heard that Pellazgu of Cairo, which has always shown itself to be a genuinely Albanian organ, is going to provide you with assistance. I have no doubt that our patriots will give proof of unity and fraternity.

I remain, faithfully yours,

Faik Konitza

P.S. I appreciate what you wrote about the *'national side of things'* and am happy that you liked the programme. As soon as I hear from America that things are underway, I will let you know so that you can publish the charts in time. I regret to say it, but the support you gave to the Agimi alphabet with your work was not well looked upon by many Albanians.

[Posted in London on February 3, 1908]

AQSH. f.44. d.21.page 123

[23] London, March 14, 1908

translated from Albanian by Robert Elsie

To Lef Nosi

Dear Lef,

I was pleased to read your letter which I received yesterday. I replied to your last letter which you sent me five months earlier, on the day of receipt, as requested. It was returned to me in the mail because you did not go and pick it up. It would be a sad thing for someone not to pick up his mail out of pure indolence, but for someone travelling on business, his friends should not pay attention to such details. I will therefore wait until I hear from you again and will, in the meantime, send you back the returned letter which I have not opened.

Not knowing whether or not you will receive this letter, I will leave what I wanted to write for another time.

I was surprised and delighted to read the article in '*Kombi*'.
How are your eyes now?

I remain, yours faithfully,

Faik Konitza

The addresses of L. Gurakuqi. and Mr. Alessandro Giovanni are:
Signor Luigi Guracucchi, Piazzetta Olivella, Naples, Italy

Signor Alessandro Giovanni, Professore di lingua albanese à San Adriano, San Demetrio Corone, Cosenza, Italy.

AQSH. f.32. d.55. page 162

[24] London, October 14, 1908

translated from Albanian by Robert Elsie

To That Splendid Patriot,
His Excellency,
Dervish Bey Elbasani

Dear Dervish Bey,[13]

I was very pleased by the high opinion you expressed of me in the letter I received recently. I have been away from London for three or four weeks. From another letter I received today from Elbasan, I see that the Bashkim Society you spoke of was established and is advancing well. I have no doubt that with such an ardent patriot as yourself and with other patriots, Elbasan is bound to play an important role in Albanian affairs. As Mr Lef Nosi, whom I have met on many occasions here in London, can tell you, I dream that Elbasan will become the capital of Albania.

Some time ago, a friend of mine, Mr Brailsford, published an article in the Times in praise of Mehdi Bey Frashëri, whom he met in Ohrid. This will doubtless help Mehdi Bey with the new government. It is probably that he will become the *'mutasarrif'* (governor) in a few months' time.

I trust that this letter will find you in good health.

Faik Konitza

AQSH. f.69. d.5. pages 29-30

[25] October 27, 1908

translated from Albanian by Robert Elsie

to Lef Nosi

3, Oakley Crescent,
City Rd, E.C.

Dear Friend,

In a letter A. Xhuvani sent me several days ago, he said that we (you and I) are now getting along and that the *"alphabet question will be solved very soon."* I do not believe that we are strong enough to give satisfaction to our friend to ..... Nonetheless, to make things clear, I believe that better could not have been done. Alas, the fate of Albania is such that there will never be progress in that country. Everything which has been said seems to have been in vain. The enemies of civilisation have rushed to the fore to close the door on reason, judgment and an exchange of ideas.

The Qiriazis and others have declared in the papers that they intend to hold a congress in Manastir [Bitola]. They say that whoever wishes to attend may do so. This means that if 20 people like yourself, who have dealt with the issue, attend, their opinions will be of no avail if 21 manual labourers and peasants, who are of a different opinion, also attend. Has there ever been a literary congress that was not a waste of time? Whoever wishes to attend may do so! No question here of delegates chosen in accordance to criteria and invited. There is no working agenda. Whoever wishes to attend may do so! Should 200 soldiers coming back from Baghdad happen to pay a visit upon the Kyriasis and vote for a certain alphabet, then this one will be chosen as the national alphabet! I believe this is the first time that a literary problem has ever been solved by a simple majority vote. Poor Albania, where people like Kyriasi, Shahin and Pekmezi are considered to be individuals of importance.

My friend, I do not believe that your reputation will suffer if you fall out with such individuals. Their haste and methods, not even allowing enough time for those abroad to attend and for word to spread as to what is actually to take place at such a congress, lead one to suspect that they are afraid of an exchange of opinions and are endeavouring to win by trickery. I can assure you that their deeds will enter the annals of Albanian history as among the most base and ignominious ever.

But you must not forget something else. If you want to make Elbasan the capital of Albania, as we have stated so often, you must realize, my friend, that the alphabet question must be solved in Elbasan. A problem of national importance must be discussed and solved in the national capital. We must never recognize Manastir as our capital.

I hope you received the letter I sent you from Eastbourne. It was actually your turn to write, but I wanted to get the letter off with no delay.

I hope that you arrived safe and sound and everyone was at home to welcome you back. I have much to tell you, but will leave it for another time.

Yours faithfully,

Faik Konitza

AQSH. f.32. d.55. pages 165

[26] February 10, 1913

To the British Foreign Office

Memo

The Powers have agreed on the principle of the independence of Albania. The point now under discussion is the question of the boundaries of the new state. Russia is trying hard to make Albania as small as possible by inducing the Powers to cede to Serbia and Greece large regions inhabited either exlusively or in great majority by Albanians. The Albanians are convinced that their case would receive the kind consideration of the British Government, of the Englishmen in general, and of the Catholics in particular, if the situation were better understood.

Catholic Sympathies

Most of the Albanian lands claimed by Servia & Montenegro (viz. Prizren, Ipek, Scutari, the Malesia) are inhabited by Catholics. The Albanians are the only Catholics to be found in the Balkans; and since to the end of 17th century the Catholic religion was called in the Servian language *'the Albanian religion'* (cf. *'Cuneus Prophetarum'*, by the Archbishop Bogdani, Venice 1692). Russia, by having the Catholics of Albania annexed to Servia, aims at the extinction of Catholicism in the Balkans. The Servians will try by all means to compel the Catholics to leave the Church. The Servians have always persecuted the Catholics. A French monk of the 14th century, Friar Brochard (quoted by Miss Mary E. Durham[14] in her book on Northern Albania) has left a terrible picture of the systematic crimes of Servia to force the Albanian Catholics to become schismatics. The Albanians of the U.S.A. recalled this painful historic fact in the following cable to His Holiness:

Boston, Mass. November 18, 1912.
To His Holiness the Pope, Rome.

Holy Father, - The Albanians of America, belonging to different creeds, held in Boston a Convention where they decided to beg your Holiness, as the highest moral authority on earth, to use Your influence to prevent the spoliation and partition of Albania, a country which gave to the Church a saint like Saint Jerome[15], a Pope like Clement XI[16] and the glorious champion of Christendom, Georg Castriot Scanderbeg[17]. The Servians and Greeks who now want to divide Albania are descendants of thouse compelled the greatest part of the Albanian people to leave the Holy Roman Church. Begging Your benediction for Albania, we cry: Long live Your Holiness!

(signed)
Fr. F. Noli[18], Orthodox Priest
Fr. N. Cere,
Faik Bey Konitza

If the Albanian Catholics are separated from Albania and annexed to Servia and Montenegro, all the work done for fifteen years to prepare the gradual return of all Albania to the Catholic Church would be lost. The Albanians, whether Moslem or Orthodox, know that they are so through a misfortune, that their ancestors were all Catholics and have fought years for their faith before being conquered by the sword of the Turk. The esteem in which the Albanian Catholics are held by their countrymen is shown by the fact that, in the Provisional Government sitting at Vallona, the Minister of Justice is a Catholic prelate, Monsignor Kachorri. By losing her Catholic population, Albania would lose a living example and a continual rememberance of their ancestral religion.

English Sympathies

1.) In all the books written by English travellers previous to the Slavonic propagandas, the writers lay great stress on the superiority of the Albanian character, morals, honour, and intellegence as compared with the Greeks, the Servians, the Montenegrins and the Bulgarians.

2.) In such popular and recent books as Murray's Guide to Greece (where there is an appendix concerning Albania) it is said that there is much in the Albanians to appeal to Englishmen, their character being nearer to the character of the English than that of any other nation.

Why should Albania become the victim of Russian intrigues, when, if given a chance, she is likely to become a better country than her neighbours? If she lacks experienced men, she may engage foreign advisers, - and certenly she has more energy than the Servians or the Greeks.

III. The British Government's Sympathies

In 1880, Lord Goschen[19] and Lord Fitzmaurice[20] advised the British Government to assist in the liberation of the whole of Albania, such an assistance and such a liberation being in the permanent interests of England. The Albanians hope that their position is still unchanged. If to-day they are rather the protégés of the Triple Alliance, their admiration and friendly feeling for England are as vivid as in the time when they helped the British Government against Napoleon's intrigues in the Mediterranean. The stronger Albania shall be, the abler will she be to stand by herself without relying on powerful neighbours and being obliged to become their instrument.

Yours sincerely,

Faik Bey Konitza

PRO. FO371/1769

[27] Baadgastein, June 22,1913

To Aubrey Herbert

Hotel Bellevue, Badgastein

Dear Mr. Herbert,[21]

Although it is a long time since I left London, I have always kept in touch with the Albanian delegates and know all the generous work you have done for our cause. I am sorry I could not stay in London to try and help in my modest way my friends the delegates. But I had to go to the Trieste Congress[22], of which I was elected the chairman.

Since the Congress I have done some work in Vienna and Berlin, and now I am going to Rome, to see the Marquis di San Giuliano.[23] Later, I intend paying a visit to Scutari, where I have many friends. I would like very much to take advantage of this opportunity of meeting Admiral Burney, whose name will have some place in the history of the Albanian state. Is it presuming too much on your kindness if I ask you to get me a letter of introduction for the Admiral? My address is Hotel Michel, Rome.

Hoping you will excuse the intrusion,

I remain yours faithfully,

Faik Konitza

SRO DD/DRU 33

[28] Rome, July 20th 1913

To Aubrey Herbert

Dear Mr. Herbert,

On my return from a trip in the country, I found your kind letter with introduction to Admiral Burney.[24] I thank you sincerely. I am leaving Rome to-morrow. On Tuesday evening I shall be in Durazzo. I hope to see you in Scutari, where I think I will be by the 5th of the August.

The Marquis di San Giuliano had received me very nicely. He seems anxious to give Albania good frontiers in the South, but I have great misgivings.

I have met here Essad Pasha[25]; the defender of Scutari. He told me he would pay shortly a private visit to Scutari, so you may meet there this interesting individual.

With high regards,

yours faithfully,

Faik Konitza

SRO DD/DRU 33

[29] Durazzo, Albania. November 18, 1913

To Aubrey Herbert

Dear Mr. Herbert,

I received your nice letter, but being away in places where there are no post-offices I could not write you sooner. I am sorry to hear that you have been seriously ill, and hope you now are restored to health.

I met Mr. Bourchier[26] in Scutari. He came with Mr. Levenon Gower[27] and I to Durazzo. They went on with Mehmed Bey[28] to Tirana and Kruja and were received well everywhere although not, of course, as enthusiastically as was the case when you came. Bourchier, who afterwards went to Valona, Berat, Elbassan, etc., is very enthusiastic about Kruja.

I had yesterday a stormy conversation with Essad Pasha, and a complete (I cannot yet say a definitive) rupture followed. The reason is as follows:

It came to my knowledge that, by secret arrangement with Essad the prince William zu Wied[29] was to land yesterday at Durazzo and have himself proclaimed by surprise. Now Essad Pasha has acted so foolishly towards the Catholics since he assumed a power on the 12th of August that the coming at this moment of protestant prince under the patronage the Essad would be tantamount to the declaration of civil war.

I believe the Prince Wied must come, on two conditions:

1st. after winning the good will of Albanian Catholics through the medium of such men as the archbishop of Scutari celebrated poet Father Gjergj Fishta[30], and businessmen such as Stef Tzuran[31], Suma[32] and Choka[33], all of Scutari

2nd. he should land, as Mr. Bourchier puts it, *"with the prestige of all Europe"*, that is to say not secretly (as would have been easily done two month ago), but with pomp, with an international fleet accompanying him, and so on. Otherwise there will be endless trouble.

I enclose a list of the books I have asked you for. I believe however that I have added one or two names. I shall refund the difference.

Yours very sincerely,

Faik Konitza

SRO DD/DRU 33

[30] Bucharest, Jan. 21, 1914

To Aubrey Herbert

My dear Mr. Herbert,

The life I am leading - that of a wandering Jew - prevented me from sending you my new year compliments. I was just then on my way from Vienna to Bucharest, where I had been invited to come and give my opinion about the future of the Wied dynasty in Albania. The King, and the Queen of Rumania, aunt of Prince Wilhelm, received me very nicely, and we had a long chat. Things do not look very promising just now in Albania, but I think it is undeniable that the bulk of the population wants peace and order and know full well that they cannot get it except through an Occidental dynasty.

My younger brother writes me from Durazzo that a parcel of books arrived for me. I expect it was from you. I thank you very much; it is a very generous contribution to my collection of educational books from different countries. I want to have as many as possible either translated or adapted for use in Albanian schools.

Hoping to see you by and by in Albania (and why not as British Envoy? No Englishman is more popular than you among the Albanians...),

I remain yours very sincerely,

Faik Konitza

PS I go back to Vienna tomorrow.

SRO DD/DRU 33

[31] Lausanne, November 2, 1915

translated by Mandy Belster

Germany and Albania

An open letter to Hans Delbrück,[34] government advisor and lecturer in modern history at the University of Berlin.

Sir,

A group of Albanian patriots has given me the task of writing to you to ask you a question. I am taking this opportunity to put to you a few personal thoughts at the same time.

Some French newspapers have recently reproduced a conversation which you are alleged to have had with an editor from the New York American. Among other quotations attributed to you is the following: *'As we have stated, Germany wants to free the small nationalities in this war.'*

This, Sir, would be a nice change in your national habits, for what Prussia's moral grandeur has always lacked is the ability to take an interest in the fate of the meek. But on the other hand, the existence has just been announced of a Bulgarian-Greek treaty for the sharing out of Albania, a treaty which was suggested, approved, licensed and guaranteed by Germany. And it is on this point, Sir, that I am taking the liberty of asking you a question at the request of my compatriots: how do you reconcile your noble declaration with the brutal plan to dismember Albania?

This is a country, a people who fit into the category of *'small nationalities'*, and who deserved your particular goodwill and respect. Did your Mommsen[35] not say that the Albanian nationality is the most ancient in the Balkans? Did your Virchow not often call Albania the *'truly superior'* nationality of Eastern Europe? Have not your intellectuals always repeated that we are a people apart, from a powerful stock, distinct from its neighbours both by its language and its mentality? Did your diplomats not defend, at the London conference, the right of the Albanian nationality to exist, did they not sign the protocol which rewarded their efforts? This *'scrap of paper'* is scarcely a day old, and the ink with which your plenipotentiary signed his name is scarcely dry. Has Albania suddenly stopped being a nationality, or stopped being small? In fact, what are these "small nationalities" which you are going to *'free'*? Is it Belgium and Poland? Serbia, perhaps? Please, Sir, kindly satisfy our curiosity and tell us which!

* * *

Germany's dealings with regard to the Albanians are particularly hateful, if we consider the events which took place in Albania during and after the Balkan war. The Serb invasion and everything that went with it, are too notorious to require a reminder. But it is good not to forget what the Serbs used to say then, and have never stopped repeating since: they justified their excesses by declaring that they had nothing against us in as far as we were Albanian, but that they were obliged to fight the *'friends and protégés of the Swabians in us.'* Thus the Germans became the indirect, but definite cause of our sorrows.

However, during the long suffering which had befallen us, one hope eased our hearts: the arrival of a leader who was capable of thought and action. Prussia didn't take long to fulfil our hopes, sending us that Messiah in the form of a six foot giant, polite, smiling (even when there was no reason to smile), and as good-natured as possible, but who was unequalled for simple-mindedness in the whole area from Neman to the Rhine and from Lübeck to Passau. What an incredible stroke of bad luck! In a country which was prey to intrigue and factions, and which needed a clear thinker with a firm hand in order to save it and guide it, Prince Wilhelm zu Wied came to add his incoherence and worsen the disorder.

Finally, one fine day, Dr von Jagow,[36] chief of Berlin police, landed in Durazzo. A guest of the prince's, he was bringing advice, and this advice was followed. That same night, pieces of ordnance were put in position around the approaches to the palace, and at dawn they vigorously bombarded the house in which the Prime Minister, a man who was neither sentenced nor even committed for trial, and still invested with his power, was gently sleeping with his wife. The consequences of this act of unintelligent authoritarianism are only too well known.

We had imagined that we had finished with the Germans. However, here was Field-Marshal Makensen[37] entering the Balkans at the head of his armies. Immediately, the naive Albanians took to arms and rebelled, in order to attract and hold part of the Serb forces who were fighting against the invasion. Others, who were enrolled in the Serb army and who had previously been resigned to their fate, deserted en masse so as not to be obliged to shoot against German and Austro-Hungarian soldiers. The Albanian people thus risked harsh reprisals, and were well aware of this. But they thought that they were making sacrifices for their liberation. They didn't yet know that the invaders were bringing definitive servitude, nor that German bugles would play the funeral march of the ancient Illyrian nation, respected for twenty centuries by the Roman and then Byzantine emperors, and then the Sultans.

* * *

It goes without saying, Sir, that you feel no hatred for us. It would be absurd to suppose this. There are other reasons to explain your conduct, and it is easy to discern at least two of these.

The four grey women whom Goethe[38] talks about in his Second Faust, have just penetrated Germany. Vier graue Weibe treten auf. They are coming forward and introducing themselves. *"I am called Famine"*, says the first, *"I am called Debt"*, says the second, *"I am called Worry"*, says the third, *"I am called Distress"*, says the fourth. The four grey ladies are the unwelcome visitors that one rids oneself of at any price. But how to go about it? Only gold could keep them away, but there is none. The Minister Helfferich, who is learned, found a solution, precisely in that Second Faust which we have just mentioned.

The Second Faust opens with a scene at the imperial court, with no further detail. The Emperor and his counsellors are deliberating on the economic crisis which is sweeping across the Empire. One minister declares that the public wealth has been eroded by wars, another complains about the cost of living. They all admit that the situation is desperate. They decide, in the absence of anything better to do, to feign optimism, to appear to have faith in the future, and to give everyone the impression that they were in a period of plenty by holding a bit public festival. The festival is successful, but after this empty show, harsh reality is all the more poignant. However, suddenly, the Marshal enters joyfully and announces that everything is going very well. The General comes to say that the troops have been paid, the Treasurer exclaims that the coffers are overflowing with riches

"So it's a miracle?" asks the Emperor

"Not at all" says the Treasurer, *"While you were presiding at the festival, dressed up as great Pan, your Chancellor said: 'I bet that all I need is a few strokes of the pen to make everybody happy.' So, for the rest of the night, a thousand artists quickly copied a few notes written in his hand, which said simply: 'This piece of paper is worth ten, this one a hundred, this other one a thousand ' and so on. Your signature is also on all these pieces of paper. Since then, all the people have been joyful… the Empire is saved.'*

"What!" says the Emperor, *"Do my subjects take this for real money? Are the army and the court content to be paid in this way? It's a miracle I cannot admire enough."*

Dr Helfferich has just renewed this miracle which was worthy of imperial admiration, by an expedient which is almost identical to that used by the chancellor in the Second Faust:

Zu wissen sei es jedem, der's begehrt:
Der Zettel hier ist tausend Kronen wert.
Ihm liegt gesichert, als gewisses Pfand,
Unzahl vergrabnen Guts im Kaiserland
Nun ist gesorgt, damit der reiche Schatz,
Sogleich gehoben, diene zum Ersatz.

Unfortunately, in the Second Faust, as in real life, this clever dodge has a tragic end. Because, although treaties are only sometimes *'pieces of paper'*, bank-notes always are if the gold reserve which they are supposed to represent is imaginary or too small.

It is well known in Germany that bankruptcy is inevitable, unless rapid and decisive successes obtain an indemnity from the defeated side which could redeem her. So any idea of establishing a definitive, or even a lasting political situation has been abandoned. It is in vain that they are still making a show of enthusiasm, for clear-sighted men will not mistake the fever of panic for ardour. Germany by now has only one goal: **Peace** - even a peace without honour, so long as it is a peace with money. And, to make this passionate desire come true, they are hiring auxiliaries at any cost, giving what they have and what they don't have, even giving up principles which had been set at the beginning of the war as fundamental ones of vital importance.

For example, they used to declare in those days that it was important to prevent the formation of a large Yugoslav monarchy by suppressing Serbia as an independent state, which will one of these days be bordering the Adriatic and set on the only seaside route from Austria. Now, these Germans who have political ability must know that if Bulgaria inherits some Serb territories, it will also sooner or late inherit the Serb programme. It is its geographical and military position which will make it, even despite itself, the champion of the Southern Slavs. When time has healed resentments, will Bulgaria be able to resist the logic of circumstances for long, once it is solicited by Yugoslav nationalists and encouraged from elsewhere?

There was a time when England, as Germany does today, wanted to prevent a Slav majority in South Eastern Europe. She waged the Crimean war with this aim in mind. She tore up the treaty of San Stefano, and dragged Russia to the Berlin Congress. She chopped up with large swipes of the scissors Count Ignatieff's[39] Great Bulgaria. Her diplomats studied the problem of the balance of power in the Balkans. In 1880, Lord Goschen, the British ambassador in Constantinople, suggested the creation of a great Albania, which was to stretch from Mitrovitza to Salonika, as a necessary counterweight to the Slav expansion. That is what it is to have clear political vision, lucid ideas, rigorous thoughts.

The Germans could have taken lessons from these masters of diplomacy. But, having adopted the old English policy of fighting the Slav dominance in the Near East, the Germans abandoned it even before they had begun it. Serbia was to be annexed to Bulgaria - and what does this mean, other than that instead of two small Slav states, enfeebled by rivalry, their union would give rise to one Slav kingdom, vigorous and disciplined, capable of putting forward a million excellent soldiers?

As if this were not enough, Albania was to be added to these vast territories, so that the future Southern Slav empire would extend from the Black Sea to the Adriatic. Faced with this outcome, is the blindness of mediocre diplomacy sufficient to explain Germany's contradictory policy in the Balkans? If one does a U-turn, if one turns one's back on the main aim of a war, it can only be done wittingly. And only driving need can make one abandon a policy which has already cost so much of its proponents' blood. The motive is fear of bankruptcy. Economic reasons come before any other consideration. One gives up on moral and political victory, one gives up on guarantees of a premeditated, long term re-drawing of the map. All one wants is an indemnity, and the sooner the better.

* * *

It is clear that, above all else, Albania has the failing of being friendless and defenceless, and of being where it is, an easy gift placed along an important route. And she has another failing, which is considerable in the eyes of the Germans; that of being tiny in size.

No, Professor, no small nationality will owe its liberation to you. You are too concerned with quantity to take an interest in a little particle. Your ethics are very strange - they have their origin in numerical science, and are merely a branch of statistics. Moral values and human dignity in themselves do not exist for you. As the chivalrous country of France has 40 million inhabitants against 90 million Germans from the allied empires, a

Frenchman is scarcely worth half a German, and a single German is worth eleven Belgians. And a whole Albanian is worth exactly a fortieth fraction of a German. Can you reasonably condescend to bother yourself with a people who are simply worth one of your fingers, or your thumb?

And yet, this arithmetical method of viewing moral problems has its drawbacks: it often misled your diplomats' judgement. Bismarck[40] said *"Bulgaria is not worth the bones of a Pomeranian grenadier"*. And in a way that is true, for today Bulgaria has proven that she is worth the bones not just of one, but of several thousand German soldiers. Another historical anecdote: the Boers, encouraged by Berlin, declared war against the English, but when, after their defeat, President Krüger visited Berlin, a pathetic and vulnerable supplicant, this defeated chief of a handful of peasants was shown the door. Moreover, as should have been predicted, and in response to your recent manoeuvres to include the Boers in your game, general Botha showed you the door in his turn and gave your callousness the lesson it deserved.

You could draw one lesson from these representative examples: that your long-sightedness leaves something to be desired, and that the errors of judgement of yesterday should warn you against taking any hasty decisions today.

Yours respectfully,

Faik Konitza

CAS. D.D. Archive

[32] February 5, 1915

translated by Robert Elsie

To Mme Parashqevi Qiriazi[41]

5/3 Rathausstraße, I
Vienna

Dear Madame,

I received your letter some time ago, but I was unfortunately not able to write to you before. I hope you will forgive me.

Since you left Vienna, there have been many changes in the dynasty which has been ruling in Albania. Princess Sophia, who remained neutral for some time, turned her back on the patriots and easily joined those parasites who were aiming at destroying Albania and would try it again if Albania were to rise once more and we would be free to act. For this reason, I regard it as an act of patriotism not to have anything more to do with Princess Sophia and her husband. But you should, of course, do whatever your conscience tells you.

Hoping to have the pleasure of reading another of your letters, I would ask you to convey my best wishes to Mr Christo Dako.[42]

Yours faithfully,

Faik Konitza

AQSH. f47. d14. pages 4-5

[33] 25 April 1916

translated by Peter Rennie

To Dervish Bey Biçaku (Elbasani)

Hotel Frauenhof, 4 Josefsplatz
Baden, near Vienna

Dear Bey,

A few days ago your letter was delivered, and I was surprised to see that you are astonished by my silence. On the contrary, I wrote to you four times, and I made repeated efforts to get my letters to you; but the Ottoman Embassy refused, with the least possible politeness, to receive them: I had thought that at least you would have heard of my efforts. Evidently, Hilmi Pasha has original ideas on the duties of a diplomat; he probably does not know that all other ambassadors, here or elsewhere, consider it their duty to accept every document addressed to their governments when the bearer tells them it is important and urgent; to make more sure my letters would be transmitted I sent them to you at the Ministry of Foreign Affairs.

And to think that this is wartime! But let us suppose that someone possesses information about a revolution being prepared against the security of the Ottoman Empire and that he wants to warn the Cabinet or the government party, with Hilma Pacha's system that would be absolutely impossible. Happily, I had nothing serious to transmit, and after having visited the doorkeeper at the Embassy for a month to no avail I had finished by renouncing writing to you.

The tragic death of poor Tufektchieff, so devoted to Turkey and to our cause in general, has afflicted me profoundly. He had telegraphed me of his next arrival, and two days after this message he fell, victim of his friendship for us. It is an irreparable loss, for I know that Tufektchieff's influence was really very great despite the enemies he had, and besides he was an idealist who knew how to devote himself to an idea. This tragic death and the attitude of the Ottoman Embassy in Vienna made me fear that you had renounced our programme. Nevertheless, as I was too advanced to withdraw, I continued without hesitation the work I had begun. And I am going to tell you briefly how matters are.

I have brought together here all those that I could: Nuzhet Bey Vrioni, who came from Brunn in Moravia where he lives, Dervish Hima[43] and several others less known, such as Imanizade Redjep Effendi, Djelal Bey, etc. and we have talked. I was a little afraid of pro-Austrianism among some of our comrades, but they all behaved correctly. We have formed a sort of initiative committee, and I am happy to declare that we have found only one adversary, Sureya Bey, who prefers to bark with the Catholics; our Muslim students are particularly enthusiastic, which is a good sign.

I have gone twice to Budapest and I shall send Dervish Hima there again in a little while. There are many Albanian merchants in Hungary who go there on business since Trieste and other Mediterranean markets are closed to them. I have spoken to several of them as on their return to Albania they can undertake active propaganda. One of these brave men was so happy when I gave him the hope, God willing and if we bestir ourselves, of having a Turkish prince that he kissed my hand with tears in his eyes. This is to show you that the idea is truly popular.

I did something else in Budapest. I looked up an old journalist there, Ármin Sasvári,[44] currently assistant director of the Commercial Museum of Budapest. I told him that the Albanian people wanted an Ottoman prince as sovereign, and to impose any other would be altogether an injustice and a political mistake. Could not Mr. Sasvári write a brochure in Hungarian on these lines? I would put at his disposal all necessary funds for the printing cost and author's rights. One could also, a little time afterwards, publish a German translation of the brochure. Mr. Sasvari asked me for two days to think about it, and two days later he came to tell me that he had accepted, and had already drawn up a plan for the brochure. He read it to me, warning that he wrote like a Magyar, and that consequently he had to observe a certain reserve and not defend our cause loudly but with subtlety. I entirely approved, and after having proposed several corrections and additions, which he noted immediately, I handed him several banknotes on account, and returned to Vienna for the second time.

On my first visit here, arriving from Constantinople, I paid visits to the Ministry of Foreign Affairs and the Ministry of War. I was received politely, but with marked coolness. I found little eagerness there to approve our point of view, although no hostility. Ten days or so after my arrival from Budapest for the second time, I had a phone call in my hotel asking me to go the next day to the Ministry of Foreign Affairs for a talk, which I did. Complaining about my growing agitation for a Muslim prince, and after many friendly compliments and also several scarcely disguised threats for my future in Albania, they begged me to cease agitating; I was assured, moreover, that they were not in favour of any other prince, that they were loyally in favour of independence for Albania, but to pose already the question of a future sovereign would be to create a state of mind from which Italy and the Entente would profit.

I objected, however, that the Prince of Wied was in Vienna, that I had met him twice on the Ring and that he had looked angrily at me; his agent Sureja Bey and his Catholic and Orthodox supporters were making open propaganda and nobody criticised them. They promised to stop all agitation and that the Prince of Wied and his supporters would soon leave Vienna. I thanked them and said that we have never wanted to make hostile agitation with regard to Austria-Hungary, but only desired, with the aid of Austria-Hungary and her allies, to resolve the problem of Albanian sovereignty in the sense of the will of the people; and that we are united with the Turks by religious links, the fact of a common religious head and also by family ties following continuous intermarriages for the past five hundred years, and that it is therefore natural to look towards Constantinople; moreover, the Ottoman government has not given us any encouragement; only we have taken the initiative for a movement, having every reason to believe that the Central Powers regard our action with a favourable eye.

These vague assurances do not seem to have inspired much confidence; for several days later, when I wanted to go to Brno to see some Albanians there, the police made some difficulties. What alarmed the Austrian government to this extreme is probably telegrams from Albania announcing the success of the idea which we have sown through our emissaries. The business of the Budapest brochure may also have annoyed the Austrians who do not want to excite Hungarian opinion. In any case, on returning to my hotel, I found Armand Sasvari, who told me: *"I come from Budapest to tell you that the Hungarian censor has authorised the publication of my brochure; the text is printed and I bring you the proofs. Here they are. But I must tell you that the Ballplatz is angry. It would be better to remove the passages touching on the question of a sovereign and to say only that Islam is awaking everywhere, in Albania as elsewhere, and that one has to take account of this fact."* I understand that Sasvari had already decided to modify the brochure and that it was useless to speak to a man of bad faith. I said to him: *"Do as you want."*

I have begun to think about the deep causes of this unexpected hostility on the part of Austria and have tried to pierce this mystery. There may be several secondary causes, but I think what Austria fears above all is giving a bad example to Bosnia. And then there is this: if the war ends, Austria without territorial advantage for the Habsburg monarchy would want to throw to public opinion the consolation of having consolidated the freedom of the Adriatic by sending a trustworthy prince of its own choice to Albania. Who this prince is, I still cannot say.

To resume, the affair from the popular point of view is going well and gaining ground; from the diplomatic point of view it is meeting difficulties. The Swiss frontier still being closed for several weeks because of troop movements, I am forced to remain here in Austria. We shall work within the bounds of possibility. Have the goodness to send me a word that my present letter has reached you, and believe me, my dear Bey, your sincere and devoted

Faik Konitza

AQSH. f13. d3. p.age 45

[34] 6 September 1916

translated by Peter Rennie

To Dervish Bey Biçaku (Elbasani)

Vienna VIII
Langegasse No.26, Tur 11,

My dear Bey,

I have received your letter in time, and if I have delayed writing to you, it is because I have had serious difficulties.

I am completely in agreement with what you write on how we should act with regard to the Austrians: it is evident that we treat and win them to our point of view rather by gentleness and persuasion than by violent opposition, which would not have any chance of success at this moment. It is just as well that I have started it early. But the Austrians are so sensitive over this question of a Turkish prince for Albania that they regard it as a hostile act even to voice such an opinion. And to show that they do not wish to allow anyone taking up this question, on 19th July the government sent detectives to search my home in Baden: they removed all my papers; happily I had kept nothing compromising, and they returned them several days later.

About the same time that my home in Baden was being searched, several Muslim officers were arrested in Albania. Five of these officers were shot. Naturally, some reason to justify these measures had to be invented. But in Albanian circles it was said that their only crime was to have had Turkish sympathies.

It is certain that there is a movement in the country in support of our programme. But the Austrian government exaggerates its importance. What is more probable - and all my information tends to show this - is that a group of young Austrian officers, with the complicity of some Albanians, organised extensive blackmail and payment for protection. The execution of the five officers, by spreading terror, has naturally increased the number of people ready to buy security. To give you an idea of the corruption prevailing in the Austrian occupying force in Albania here are several small facts:

Every traveller going to Scutari must give a tip at Cattaro of 60 crowns to continue his journey. In Albania, a Turkish gold pound is exchanged by the Austrian authorities for 22 paper crowns, a gold napoleon for 19 paper crowns - this is theft pure and simple since on the Vienna exchange a Turkish pound is worth more than 32 crowns and a napoleon more than 30. If the government buys something from the peasants it pays them in Austrian banknotes; but with these same notes, the peasants cannot buy anything from the government, which only wants to receive gold. The Wiener Bank Verein itself in Scutari does not accept Austrian crowns. The government gives the population two kilos of maize and exacts five kilos of oil as payment. I could continue, but these examples will suffice.

If, after this, the Austrians have not a single friend in Albania, they have only themselves to blame. Even the Catholics are now against Austria. And this at the moment when Italy is preparing an attempt to advance towards the north! Only the influence of Turkey at a given moment could save the situation. But the Austrian government, which is not aware of the situation, does not want to hear talk of Turkish influence. Moreover, it considers the actual regime in Turkey as feeble and transitory.

As you can see from the attached telegram which Professor Baron von Dungern had just sent me, several friends of our cause wanted to see me in Germany, and I was expecting much from this visit, but the Austrians prevented me from going. My situation, which was more important than that of every other Albanian in Austria, has become detestable since my return from Constantinople. Austria wants thus to make an example.

All my friends are holding firm. I regret mentioning only one exception: Dervish Hima. Tufektchieff did not like him, and had dissuaded me from taking him with me. Unfortunately, I did not heed this advice. At first,

Dervish Hima behaved well. And then, suddenly, he began to sidestep. I believe he went to the Ministry of Foreign Affairs to say what he knew, happily he did not know everything. However, I had not left him lacking anything, knowing his weakness: I had given hin 200 Turkish pounds for his expenses!

Regarding this, I must say that the sum which Tufektchieff sent me has been spent. He had to put at my disposal a new sum on his arrival in Vienna. Lacking funds, it will be difficult to continue propaganda. It is true that just now we cannot do much.

Be pleased to accept, my dear Bey, the assurance of my high regard and sincere devotion,

Faik Konitza

P.S. My dear Bey, the Ottoman Consul General in Vienna has written to the Ministry of the Interior in Constantinople to ask permission to endorse the passport of Emine Hanoum Toptani[63], relative and enemy of Essad who wants to go to Switzerland where his brother-in-law has just died. I would be profoundly obliged if a favourable reply could be hastened. I have been six months a *'mussafir'* in his house.

AQSH. f13. d3. page 45

[35] Vienna, 7th December 1918.

To Aubrey Herbert

Dear Mr. Herbert,

I hope you and your family are well and after this long and terrible war, your health and private interests have not suffered too much.

I have been for nearly three years a civil prisoner ("konfiniert") in Austria, for having openly criticised the Austrian misrule in Albania. And during this period I have not heard anything of either family and friends.

A British officer was kind enough to promise me to take this letter to you.

To you, I beg to give or forward the enclosed letter to my brother if he is still alive.

I hope you will pardon the trouble I am giving you, and with my respectful compliments to the Hon. Mrs. Aubrey Herbert[45], I remain,

Yours sincerely,

Faik Konitza

PS.
Is your friendship for Albania still active? This poor friendless country was never more than now in need of protection. All Albania hopes that you and your friends shall not abandon her in this fateful hour. The Albanians detained in Vienna beg me to join their prayers with mine and to assure you of our undying gratitude for what you already done or will do for Albania.

SRO DD/DRU 33

[36] October 16, 1920

translated by Robert Elsie

To the Chairman of Vatra

Rome, via Thomas Cook and Sons

Dear Mr Chairman,

Yesterday, on the 15th of this month, I received a cable from you which surprised me indeed. The cable stated: *"The cables were received. Please keep up the verbal attacks on the government. Lasko is using your letters to the detriment of Vatra and of the issue at stake. Letter will follow. Anastas Pandeli."*

I sent Lasko a reply to his letter, which he had sent me fifteen months earlier. He gave me proof of his humanity at a difficult hour and I am not among those who forget a good deed, although I have often given proof myself that I can forget a bad deed. The letter I sent him was not for publication. It was private. In it, together with many other matters, I spoke of the issues of the day. It was only from Bishop Noli that I learned that Lasko was an opponent of Vatra. I had written the letter before Noli arrived here. I am sorry for any harm caused to Vatra by this misunderstanding.

s to my said *'verbal attacks'*, members of the pre-1912 Turkish government, steeped in the ways of oriental hypocrisy, have always accused me of this because they regard any expression of a free opinion as an attack. I do not think that a respected society with other ideals, such as Vatra, should bother repeating accusations made by an incriminated Turkish government against patriots. And what attacks? Did I attack the private life of some Turkish minister? Did I uncover a private scandal or some hidden shame? No, gentlemen! I am fighting for ideals and, as ardent as the battle may be, I have never deviated from public interests. If I have, I would ask you to point this out to me.

Mr Chairman, I would like to bring up a few things and give you some more explanations so that no harm is done by misunderstandings between us. In May 1919, I arrived in Italy after four years of suffering and hardship in Austria. I did so to take better care of my health and to return to Albania in order to work for the advancement of the country, no longer in politics, but simply by serving as an example, i.e. the well-spent life of a non-covetous citizen devoted to his writings and to farming.

When I arrived in Rome, I learned that Vatra had grown and was flourishing with all the vitality of a vibrant and strong society. I was overwhelmed with joy. Nonetheless, I did not give the federation any sign of life on my part. I sent it neither a wire nor a card and did not inform it of my arrival. I did not present my greetings and, even though I was in great need, it never occurred to me to ask for assistance. I remained silent, not out of indifference, but because I had put an end once and for all to my involvement in politics.

But Vatra discovered me itself. Vatra welcomed me and, with a noble gesture that I will never forget, caused me, though wearied as I was, to return to the thorny path of politics.

You may ask: Why the withdrawal from politics? I can tell you the reason very briefly. The Albanians are so unskilled in politics and so profoundly oriental that they will never be able to begin or to end a battle of ideals. We will always surround our leaders with suspicions, we will always wear them down, and will eventually kick them out and throw them into the arms of our enemies. This has happened to many figures. It is true that the Albanians in America are more skilled in politics than the others, but not enough so as to avoid mistakes. One of their errors is to believe that countries and their cabinets are the same thing, that one cannot serve one's country if the ministers of the day do not give their approval.

I have always regarded and continue to regard Vatra as an organ of the people, not as an organ of government. The Albanian people expect from Vatra enlightenment and protection on the road to advancement and not blind support for the government officials of the day. As an opponent of the government for idealistic reasons and not because of any particular dispute, I can give you a good example. Read my article in *'Dielli'*, No. 1814, page 2, written eight months ago when I was on good terms with the cabinet and was seconded on a mission to Paris. Both Sulejmani and Peci read it and said to me, *"You are using the right weapon."* I replied, *"Yes indeed, my friends. You must work like respectable individuals!"*

It is useless for me to tell you what the government is doing as you are not interested in learning the truth. But let me tell you one important thing: Vatra is on the wrong road. But so as not to make a big issue out of it, I do not intend to oppose the government any more. I will acquiesce to the policies of Vatra. I would only like the commission to know that the insults made against your deputy and the government boycott against me and against American volunteers will be severely denounced by the real people of Albania, who do not understand the patience which Vatra is showing.

Yours sincerely,
your delegate in Rome,

Faik Konitza

P.S.
I close here about an issue I raised this month with a large newspaper, Il Popolo Romano. It was printed on the 8th, i.e. six days before I received your cable. Had you informed me in good time that you did not want your delegate to oppose the, if you will, *'constitutional, legal and fair'* government, I would of course not have talked to the reporter. Unfortunately, the declaration caused a good deal of tumult in the European, and in particular Balkan press.

AQSH. f100. d26. page 4

Appollinaire, sketched by Picasso
from 'Appollinaire' by Pascal Pia, Paris, 1965

Lef Nosi (1876-1945) left

Photo by Joseph Swire in Elbasan in 1929

Reproduced by kind permission of Alexander Duma

The frontage of 4, Oakley Crescent, City Road,
in Islington, London EC1

This was both home to Faik Konitza and the office from which the 'Albanian Review' was published between 1902 and 1909.

Photo: Bejtullah Destani

Aubrey Herbert M.P. (1880-1923)
President and founder of the Albanian Commmittee (1912-1918) and later President of the Anglo-Albanian Society from 1918-1923 and champion of Albanian independence

reproduced by kind permission of Mrs Bridged Grant

Ahmet Bey Zogu,
from 1928, King Zog of the Albanians
(1895-1961)

from T. Selenica, *"Shqiperia e Ilustruar'.* Tirana,1925

Fan S. Noli (1882-1965)
Poet, writer, priest and Prime Minister of Albania for six months in 1924

reproduced from 'Faik Konitza'
Gjonlekaj Publishing Co., New York, 1995

Dervish Duma (1908-1998)
Diplomat and businessman

reproduced by kind permission of Alexander Duma

Faik Konitza (1876-1942)

[37] BOSTON 18. MASS. JANUARY, 18, 1922

To Aubrey Herbert

The Pan-Albanian Federation of America[46]
"Vatra" (The Hearth)

Dear Colonel Herbert,

Very many thanks for the five photographs. Everybody was expecting them with sympathetic curiosity, and we were wondering if you had forgotten to send them. They will be published in a few days in a weekly edition of our daily newspaper. Later on, if we can find an etcher of talent, we will have them engraved, as everybody here would like to have one.

I am busy with the work of reorganising *'Vatra'*, which Noli and I have established many years ago. It was then meant as a society for the independence of Albania. Now, I would like to turn it into a society for the political education of the Albanian people.

This is hard enough, because I have no more my first faith. I am somewhat in the position of a monk who believes no more in God or the Church, but continues to wear the frock for fear of wounding feelings of his pupils, followers and friends.

The Albanian people has some very fine qualities, and the peasantry has given of late splendid proofs of endurance, patience, love of progress and order. But a gang of crooks, grafters, spies, and upstarts has managed to occupy all the leading strategic positions in the body politic of the country and it is more than useless to try and get rid of them. Under such conditions I don't think there is much hope for the salvation of the country.

Two years ago my brother was the most popular man in Albania, and he could have succeeded in making any reform he liked. He, however, preferred to gossip in the lobbies of the Paris hotels instead of going to

Albania, and so gave a chance to lower elements, who captured the strongholds.

I came to Boston but a few days ago from Maine and must tomorrow start on a new lecturing tour to New York and Pennsylvania. So, pray excuse my bad writing, uncouth and styleless.

Tous mes respects á Mrs. Herbert.

Yours very sincerely,

Faik Konitza

SRO DD/DRU 33

[38] Washington 1938

'The Telephone Invasion of Albania'

by Faik Konitza

A week or so ago there was an Associated Press dispatch carried by *'The Times'*, to the effect that the telephone was being introduced in Albania and that up to now people have been shouting from hill to hill to spread news or carry on a conversation. There is a good deal of truth in this piece of news. The telephone has been in use in Albania for very many years, but only for military and police purposes. As a favor, and free of charge, people would be allowed now and then to send a supervised message, but that was all.

Albanians have relied for their communications on the telegraph, and sometimes two persons in different towns would sit by the side of the telegraph operators and conduct a conversation. The famous English correspondent Bourchier, known as *'the Ambassador of the Times in the Balkans',* used to say that in Albania the one efficient service, and amazingly so, was the telegraph. He was delighted to find again and again that his long dispatches in 1913 and 1914 from Albania reached always promptly and faultlessly the London office of his paper.

* * *

It is possible that the telephone may also become popular in Albania, though perhaps at the expense of public security. Seventeen months ago, an insurrection burst out in Albania and was crushed in less than twenty-four hours, mainly because the police and armed forces had telephones at their disposal, while the would-be insurgents had no such means of communication. I imagine the police will have to perfect a wire-tapping technique in order not to be caught napping.

I, for one, though from a selfish point of view, regret the telephone invasion of Albania. The telephone is a useful but irritatingly intrusive instrument. To have a telephone in your room is equivalent to giving freedom to anybody to jump up loudly in front of you and box your ears at any time of day or night. And you do not have the possibility of escape by switching off, as you do with the radio and the electric light.

A few weeks ago, one evening I was busy working on a book on Albania, when a telephone call persistently interrupted me. I unhooked it at last and a tiny voice, with a babbling of similar voices around, asked me a question. Obviously it was a party of children. The little voice said: *"Please will you tell us just where is Bilbao."* The children doubtless had looked up the embassies and legations in the telephone book and innocently had picked out the first name in the alphabetical list.

* * *

Concerning the "*shouting*" from hill to hill, as the A.P. dispatch puts it, it is true that even now it is practiced in some out-of-the-way mountains of Albania. This curious habit is of great antiquity. The English scholar, William Martin Leake[47], who traveled extensively in Albania and Greece at the end of the 18th and the beginning of the 19th centuries and published the results of his studies in several volumes, mostly in diary form, writes under the date of August 4, 1804:

"On the southern side, by which we approached the town, the position terminates in a tremendous precipice, the summit of which is so near to the church of St. George, on the opposite ridge, that words may be heard from one place to the other; and the first intelligence is constantly communicated in this manner, on the arrival of passengers or caravans, which in winter are sometimes arrested there by a sudden fall of snow for several days. It is curious to remark with how much ease this telolalia or distant conversation is carried on. It is an art, which, as well as that of teloscopia, or of distinguishing distant objects, is possessed by the Albanians and mountaineers of Greece in a degree which seems wonderful to those who have never been required

to exercise their ears, eyes, and voices to the same extent. The same qualities were among the accomplishments of the heroic ages of Greece, the manners and peculiarities of which have never been extinct in the mountainous and more independent districts of this country."

This antique means of communication has been perfected enough for travellers to order their dinner two or three hours in advance and to find on their arrival at the inn chickens or a baby lamb on the spit, or whatever else they had commanded.

(New York Times, 1938)

[39] May 31 1939

Italian Seizure of Albania Recalled

To the Editor of The New York Times

Sir:

It is an everyday experience with you to be complimented or thanked for your brilliant editorials or the excellence of your correspondences from abroad. But you will find it doubtless unique to receive, as on this occasion, a letter of sincere thanks for your appropriate use of quotation marks in a recent issue of The Times. I mean the dispatch from your Rome correspondent, published on May 30. It is said there that *"the Albanian armed forces asked to be incorporated with the Italian forces."*

Both in this text and in the headlines you put the word "*asked*" in quotation marks – a punctuation sign which has never been used more to the point. The Charlie McCarthy government of Albania has of course no voice of its own - and it would dutifully say the North Pole is contiguous to the Equator if Italy said so. But I think many people must by now have revised the heretofore prevailing opinion that the Italians as a nation are intelligent, apart from their other unflattering characteristics.

In pursuing a few thousand newspaper clippings from various countries referring to the Italian aggression against Albania, I found that "*repugnant*" is the prevailing epithet used in editorials. But apart from the moral issues, which in this case are so clear that they hardly need comment, it is interesting to study in the Albanian tragedy the type of intelligence guiding the policies of a country that calls itself great but is only large, and not very large at that.

Albanian Resistance Affirmed

First, let us take the question of the Albanian resistance. The Italians, in their hopeless desire to make the world believe that they were not aggressors but friends called in by the people for help, boldly assert that there was no resistance at all. The Albanians, on the other hand, reckon that there were around twelve thousand Italians killed, – and the Greeks, as close neighbors and observers, agree.

Let us, however, dismiss these figures as exaggerated by emotion. I have in hand letters from disinterested, neutral foreigners who happened to be in Durazzo at the time of the Italian aggression. I cannot make these letters public, but I can show them to an accredited representative of The Times. They put the number of Italian soldiers killed in Durazzo alone at a minimum of one thousand. But the Italians declare that there were only twenty-five Italian soldiers killed in the whole of Albania, and this, we are told, was done by "*bandits*" (although there were three hundred young Albanian students, almost all killed, among those resisting the invaders).

Let us for argument's sake accept this Italian figure; but we are entitled to some conclusions. As the landing took place at four points, there must have been average of six killed at each point; and as it is known beyond doubt that the Italians were several times compelled to run back to their ships, we may fairly assume that each time one soldier was killed the rest took to flight. If this is true, Italy must have sent to Albania the champion sprinters who had previously distinguished themselves at Guadalajara (Spanish Civil War).

Personal Union Analysed

Second, a few remarks about this question of Personal Union, which is supposed to be the status of Albania with regard to Italy. (I will use Personal Union and similar words with capital initials to distinguish them, as legal terms with a definite meaning, from their vague connotation in everyday speech.

What is really a Personal Union? In a recent book of scientific value, by two German scholars, ("*Hilfswoerterbuch fuer Historiker*", by Haberkern and

Wallach, Berlin, 1935), the Personal Union is defined as the union between two States which have no constitutional features whatever in common, except the person of the Sovereign. The best historic example of a personal Union is that of Great Britain with Hanover.

In contradistinction to the Personal Union, the Real Union is the union between two States which have certain constitutional features and certain authorities in common, without impairing the respective sovereignty of the two partners. The best example of a Real Union is that of Austria with Hungary.

German thoroughness is at fault in the failure of the two authors to mention a third type of union, known in Legal History as the Incorporate Union. Britain and Ireland had the Incorporate Union from 1801 to 1920. (Ireland has now practically a Personal Union with Britain.) The Incorporate Union from 1801 to outright annexation in that the weaker partner is allowed to keep certain autonomous characteristics.

Albanian Sovereignty Destroyed

It will be seen by this that Italy, by maintaining an army in Albania, by imposing fascism on the Albanians, by making the teaching of Italian compulsory, by suppressing the sound gold currency of Albania, by doing away with Albanian customs barriers, to name only a few points, not only has destroyed the Personal Union before it was born, but has not even replaced it by a Real Union: What we have is nothing else than an Incorporate Union.

The principal aim of the Italians, in insisting that the relation of Albania to Italy is one of Personal Union, is to show the English that Italy has not violated the treaty of Anglo-Italian friendship, an article of which obligated the contracting parties to respect the existing sovereignties of the Mediterranean. But they show a definite lack of intelligence in hoping to deceive the English, who more than any other nation, know what a true Personal Union is.

Previous to the Personal Union with Hannover, the English, from 1603 to

1714, had the personal Union with Scotland. When in 1603 James VI, King of Scots, became King of England, he assumed the numerical I and became James I as English King, while continuing to remain James VI as Scottish King. If Italy meant to have a sincere Personal Union with Albania, King Victor Emanuel III of Italy ought to have been proclaimed as Victor Emanuel I of Albania. The two first Victor Emanuels were not Albanian Kings. But why should gross violators of obvious rights have any regard for legal niceties?

Yours sincerely,

Faik Konitza

The New York Times, April 18, 1939

[40] December 6, 1940

To Mr. Dervish Duma[48] and Anton Logereci

1530 Sixteenth Street,
Washington, D.C.

I have the honor to acknowledge the receipt of your joint letter dated November 6, 1940, which has just reached me.

Let me first congratulate you on your estimate of Ahmet Bey Zogu[49], whom I consider a rogue and vagabond, who deserves the contempt of every patriotic Albanian. Second, let me thank you for your kindness in having thought of me as a leader of a new Albanian patriotic movement.

I am sorry to disappoint you, but I consider myself as a man aloof from politics and from now on intending to devote myself only to history and literature. But if I were inclined to meddle in politics, I certainly would not choose this moment to do so.

You both are sincere nationalists, but you both are Northerners. You cannot understand the feelings of a Southern Albanian. It has been one of the curses of Albania that sectionalism has always been a guiding principle among them. I will not bother you with references to past history to show you what Greece has done to Southern Albania. But you can get for a few shillings a copy of Miss Durham's book published in 1920 in London under the title *'Twenty Years of Balkan Tangle'*, and that will refresh your memory about the Greek atrocities in 1913: wholesale murders, systematic arson, countless rapes, even of girls under fifteen; this is the fine record of the Greeks in that year of 1913.

In the present state of South Eastern European affairs, an Albanian leader in London would of necessity have to condone all these beautiful doings of the Greeks in the recent past and in all probability in the present and near future. I know and I admit that the English are respected and liked in Albania; and this popular feeling is deep-rooted in the past: in fact, it can be shown that it goes as far as Skanderbeg's time, when the English gave not a little help to our national hero. But the hatred of the Greeks is so ingrained in the hearts of all true Albanians, that the conflict going on over there will never appear to the people as a conflict between England and Italy, but only as a conflict between Italy and Greece. Now, allow me to remind you that whatever Italy has done to Albania was of a political nature; what Greece has done to Albania was, even more than political, an aggression against the homes and the honour of the families.

I have been very frank. But please take it as a compliment to you, because your letter impressed me as serious and I did not think it proper to indulge in meaningless compliments and generalities.

Wishing you all luck and happiness, I remain,

Yours sincerely,

Faik Konitza

CAS. D.D. Archive

[41] 3rd April 1942: Copy Cable

To: Dervish Duma, East Horsley

From: Faik Konitza, Washington

Thanks for cable. Chekrezi's[50] alleged organisation merely money-making hoax. His followers only handful of men born in Albania but notorious for their hatred of Albanian nationality. You know his past and how he was dismissed for embezzlement by Albanian Government during Noli's administration. Genuine Albanians despise and avoid the man and it is a matter of surprise to me that sincere young patriots should go to the trouble and expense of even enquiring about him.

I wonder what is Zog doing? You know my opinion about his pompous incoherence and his inclination to treachery. Zog seems to me a curious mixture of two Shakespearean characters, namely, Dogberry and Iago. But Bishop Noli, whom I recently visited for a few days in Boston, succeeded in shaking my scepticism. Noli believes Zog may have learned in school of adversity and if supported by English could yet play important part as symbol of Albanian freedom.

Because of the centuries old Albanian bias in favour of England Noli thinks that a sign from the English that Zog is persona grata to them would restore much of the man's lost prestige. Most members of Vatra believe that group combining Zog, Noli and myself would be effective in compelling popular approval. Our problem for the moment is to ascertain first whether Zog has at long last learned his lesson, and second, whether His Britannic Majesty's Government are inclined to give him the benefit of the doubt and grant him their support. If both answers were affirmative, we could start something serious that might be useful for Albania and by no means useless for the Anglo-American cause.

Anyhow, I advise you to keep in touch with Bishop Noli but please don't repeat the mistake of demoting him to Father Noli. After all, he is the founder and acknowledged Bishop of a national church and at one time was the canonical Archbishop of Durazzo recognised as such even by the Greek Patriarch of Constantinople.

Please give my respects to Miss Durham, whom I consider as the first honorary citizen of Albania, and show her this cable if you like.

With kindest regards,

Faik Konitza

CAS. D.D. Archive

[42] April 2, 1942

The State Department,
Washington

My dear Mr. Konitza

I have received your letter of March 5th, and have read with close attention your remarks concerning an exchange of correspondence in the columns of the Albanian-American press, the full text of which you enclosed with your letter.

I find that Mr. Chekrezi did in fact call at the Department to discuss Albanian affairs. On that occasion the Department's views with regard to political activity concerning the affairs of foreign states were outlined, and it was emphasized that it was expected that foreign political leaders visiting the United States will not utilize the foreign language press in the United States to revive the political controversies of other countries.

Mr. Chekrezi made no mention of the incident of the closing of the Albanian legation, and I regret that there should have been an erroneous impression with regard to this matter. The Legation was, in fact, closed in the circumstances as you recall them. On June 5, 1939 the Foreign Minister of Albania notified the American Minister at Tirana that the Albanian and Italian Governments had signed an agreement whereby the diplomatic and consular services of the two countries were combined, and the Albanian Foreign Office abolished.

This Government therefore instructed the American Minister to return to the United States. Somewhat later, on June 24, in the course of your conversation with the Secretary of State, Mr. Hull stated, with an expression of regret, that in these circumstances this Government would not be in a position to continue to extend diplomatic privileges and immunities to a Minister of Albania in the United States. The formalities and technical arrangements under which the operations of the Albanian Legation were discontinued were left entirely in your hands.

With kind regards, believe me,

Very sincerely yours,

(Signed)

Sumner Welles[51],
Acting Secretary

CAS. D.D. Archive

[43] 12th June 1942.

The Old House,
West Horsley,
Surrey.

Dear Mr. Konitza,

This is not meant to be a stylish letter, but a sincere endeavour to give expression to my thoughts as they come to me and to try and concentrate on the facts.

Somehow I feel I am in a hurry and that the matter is urgently overdue. I feel I should have kept Bishop Noli and yourself informed of everything by stages as events occurred, but because in your letter of January 1940, to which we gave our utmost consideration and which we took to heart, you said you were not prepared to take part in politics at that time and because from Bishop Noli, Logoreci and I did not receive so much as an acknowledgement to our letter, we felt somewhat discouraged although we did not despair of the situation.

I hope you will not think us ungrateful for not having acknowledged your letter. I can assure you your kindness in writing to us as frankly as you did was much appreciated by both Logoreci and myself and we felt honoured that our intentions were not misunderstood by at least one elder Albanian statesman and patriot. As things were at the time, however, we agreed that there was nothing we could usefully do to further the question, but although we did not continue to correspond with you the matter was ever present in our minds. We tried to get our British friends to put forward and support our case, considering the pitiful situation in which our country was and the fear that the end of the war might find it in equally bad, if not worse, circumstances.

From your cable of 3rd April we rather gather Bishop Noli may have been offended at our addressing him as Father Noli. We did not, of course, dream of demoting and offending him - we rather foolishly but unintentionally overlooked the fact, and we assure you that he commands our highest respect. Later events have proved this, for we have held him in high esteem to our friends in England without his knowledge that we were doing so. We had hoped that he would take active part in a new Albanian movement for the restoration of Albania's independence. We did not, however, wish to press him unduly and we did not write to him again; and to this day we have not got his correct address. We hope he will accept our apologies for a genuine mistake on our part and that you will be kind enough to keep him informed of the contents of this letter.

It was so kind of you to cable me at length and to have given me what we thought was a most helpful piece of information as to Çekrezi's alleged organisation, and, above all, as to the way in which Bishop Noli, yourself and most members of the VATRA thought of tackling the question of our national cause. We were, of course, ignorant of the way Çekrezi had been running his campaign for the independence of Albania, as we were not in touch with him and at that time had not read any of his articles.

We naturally thought that he would have taken the advice of Bishop Noli and yourself as veterans and would have opened his campaign, first, to bring the Albanians together in an organised front, and secondly, to fight through the press, and otherwise, in order to gain recognition by U.S.A., Britain and the other Allies, of Albania's right to restoration of her independence at the end of the war. Only one of us, Mr. Tajar Zavalani[52] was in touch, and corresponded with, Çekrezi and I suppose that either he told us what he thought we would approve of and kept the rest to himself, or that Çekrezi purposely misled him.

When we found out and debated the question, Çekrezi had already, without even as much as asking us to nominate a representative, appointed Mr. Zavalani as his representative in London. Considering that most Albanians are ambitious, I cannot honestly tell you which one of them misled or misinformed the other but we came to the conclusion that Zavalani was either being forced, or wished to force himself to be representative of the small Albanian colony in London. And you know how difficult it is, and how long it takes for Albanians, to accept any Head unless he were of an unimpeachable character. Zavalani was thus flattered by Çekrezi and started working on his own upon Çekrezi's instructions until he found out he could make no headway.

At a meeting we held we very strongly criticised Zavalani and reminded him who Çekrezi was and what our friends in England thought of him. Thus it was that thereafter we more or less lost confidence in each other. I must say Zavalani saw his mistake and admitted it, but apologising for what he described as an unintentional blunder, continued doing things on his own unless he wanted support.

He continued writing to Çekrezi what we, the Albanians in London, were supposed to think and do without consulting us. He despatched cables over his name but by implication he led him to believe that he was speaking for all of us. You may have read in Çekrezi's paper the reports from London, most of which were all Zavalani's doing. He likes monopolising. For example, when Miss Durham was invited to speak to the Albanians on the B.B.C. the report, as it appeared in Çekrezi's paper, led people to believe that it was an agent of Zog who was going to talk and the B.B.C. did not allow her, whereas Çekrezi's representative was speaking in the name of "*Free Albania*" regularly every night. Most false and untrue statements. Zavalani is an employee of the B.B.C. and can say nothing without their approval. They in fact are unaware that he is Çekrezi's representative. The policy of the B.B.C. is not to work for different Albanian internal factions but for a united front against the invaders.

I have told you this to show you that there has been an atmosphere of distrust among the few Albanians here and to come to the more important point - that of King Zog. I maintain that he and no one else is responsible for all the misunderstandings, jealousies and discussions brought about among the Albanians here as he did in Albania, as he did in France and, to my humble opinion, as he will continue to do as long as he has the money and the vacant throne of Albania to sharpen his appetite.

To be able to appreciate fully what is to follow, I think it would be advisable for me to give you short biographical notes of who the Albanians in England are. These I attach hereto. From these you will, I hope, deduce that there are few Albanians here who can give a frank, unbiased, uninfluenced opinion on King Zog. The difficulty of procuring their livelihood in other ways, without much suffering or sacrifice, has obliged some of them to be of necessity partial. It is all a matter of means, and as no one helped us, and no one else is helping them, King Zog, being the only one with money, and with ready promises to satisfy the vanity of those who like this invisible commodity, has naturally exercised his power of influence to the full. But I must not forget to say that even then only those Albanians who put half their heart and effort to further the cause of their suffering brethren and their country can be thus influenced. And unfortunately Albania is in dire need of men - men of Bajram Curri's calibre, imbued with ancestral pride.

Consequently among the Albanians here, only a few have been in a position to speak their mind as regards Zog - Logoreci,[53] Bogdo[54], Sarachi[55], myself and lately Zavalani have been in this category, but not all of us either have been in agreement. Sarachi has been since the fall of Albania blindly and unreasonably against Zog - he who was an intimate friend of his - and one is inclined to believe that this breach has been for personal rather than national reasons. Zavalani, who came across from France with Zog and was with him here and paid by him (although I believe he never shared the King's views) had to keep on good terms until a job was found for him as broadcaster of the B.B.C. news bulletin in Albanian. He is extremely ambitious.

Bogdo, having finished his studies in Civil Engineering in England, not wishing to go back to Albania after the occupation, managed to find a job with an engineering firm in London, earning enough to keep himself alive. He is an intelligent young man with independent ideas, though perhaps a bit rash. He follows his feeling and is thus anti-Zog. Logoreci only managed to finish his studies, and got an Honours degree at the London University, after the war had begun. He was without funds. As his name will probably suggest to you he comes from a family of patriots. Zog kept all sorts of people but did not help him much. Then he was recommended and appointed as translator-broadcaster of Albanian news at the B.B.C. in

November 1940. It was really on his recommendation that Zavalani was supported to be appointed as deputy at the B.B.C. All this will explain that Zog did nothing to bring Albanians together.

And now as to myself. Contrary to your supposition, I am not a Northerner. I am from Borshi, a village which suffered the same fate as 280 others at the hands of Greek bands in 1914. In May 1939 when Mr. Kurti left the Legation and went to Switzerland, I declined to go back to Albania and on closing the Legation down managed to find employment with a British paper manufacturing firm and, together with my Albanian wife, stayed in London. My technical knowledge and my knowledge of English helped me to obtain employment and to earn my living at a time when Italy was still non-belligerent and the chances of Albanian questions coming to light were few. I still have this job and so feel independent. All my free time is devoted to my small efforts in the interests of our country.

Logoreci and I have been working together. We were school friends at the American Technical School at Tirana; we went to the same College in London, although at different times; we had the same jobs in Albania under General Percy and we have followed the same path in our national interests. We have only learned now, with the coming of Zog to England, what intrigue is. Bogdo shares our ideas and is one of us, younger, and perhaps more fiery, and with less experience.

In our service in the Albanian gendarmerie, Logoreci and I had a good opportunity of seeing all Albania, of meeting both mountaineers and townsfolk, we knew the sufferings of the people under the Zog régime, we were intimate with their complaints, and we had the opportunity of knowing King Zog as we acted as Secretary-Interpreters between him and General Percy. I was in this position from 1926 to 1932 and Logoreci from when I left to 1937. (I had the honour of meeting you at General Percy's in Tirana in 1928.) Further, since Zog has been in England I have seen him often enough to be able to form a more accomplished opinion on him. I have studied him and have been disillusioned.

I expect by now you know the whole story of Zog's last minute negotiations with the Italians, which, as expected, miscarried; of the people's desire to resist under the poor conditions he had left them; of his flight to Greece and Turkey with the coffers of gold; of his tour of Europe; of his stay in France in luxurious surroundings in fine old châteaux; of his half-hearted endeavours to start an Albanian movement there; of his escape from Bordeaux thanks to the British navy, and of his arrival to settle at the famous Ritz in London. He stayed in London a long while before, pressed by criticism of his spending right and left when Albanians were suffering both in the country and abroad for the bare necessities of life, the elephant moved to a house in the country. He went to Ascot and had a modest place, but their disproportionate sense of majesty and prestige spurred them on to materially loftier levels and so he again moved, this time to go to Lord Parmoor's palace near Henley-on-Thames - a 40-roomed building in good surroundings. Of course he has a large family with him and a number of his guards' officers and servants. These last-mentioned are good, honest, straightforward mountaineer Albanians who are pining for their homes and their families. These have been Zog's physical movements and I need not enlarge on them.

Now as to his political moves in brief: really there have been none of any national importance from the Albanian people's point of view. It is more what he has not done than what he has done that matters to us. His ways are still those of a mountaineer who in the old days had seen a bit of town life, had a little education, had some experience of wearing modern garb, as chief of a clan had had the experience of meeting a few people and made quite an interesting figure of curiosity. But when it came to understanding modern democratic political enterprise he could not see further than to deal through "*Consuls*" as in Ottoman Empire days when all intriguers of any following found refuge and advice by pleading to the "*Consuls*" of such and such a Power. He is not an educated man by any means.

His tactics are those of secret intrigue and '*divide and conquer*' as he did with the Bajraktars. He forgot he had to deal with people of straightforward ways. It surprises one because our mountaineers are men of the "*Besa*" and of pride, whose word is their bond. He has not apparently learned much during his 15 years' reign. But this is due to a large extent to the people he kept around him in high responsible positions. His advisers were men that approved all he said and, for their own ends, considered him as one who never erred, whose judgement was ever right and therefore never criticised him and he learned nothing. Besides his instinct was that of a hoarder. He collected money at all costs and at the expense of his country and his future.

Under Zog's régime there were a few things accomplished but even here the credit should go to patriots who at the risk of imprisonment, or even death, made things possible.

This was Zog as people knew him abroad. A man who had sold bits of his country to the Serbs in payment of their support for his return to Albania; one who had allowed Italy to get the country in her grasp, not for the good the country might derive from it, but for the payment in cash he would get for himself. These are facts known to all and undeniable. Such a man could not be a '*persona grata*'. Such a man should not enjoy the confidence and love of his people; he could not command respect abroad, and especially in a freedom-loving, democratic country like England. No wonder then a highly-placed British official, now a peer, described him as a tyrant.

Moreover, his enemies made such convincing propaganda against him abroad that his crimes were doubled in the eyes of the world. If they sympathised with him for a while, it was out of pity more than anything else. And when they said King Zog was no good, they, unfortunately for us, invariably coupled Albania's name with him as if Albania were his child and creation and must suffer for his sins. Not fair, but that is the true picture and we have never had enough means at our disposal to present a truer and a more proportionate one through publicity of Albania as it is, not as reflected in the person of Zog.

And yet the Albanians have at times with an abnegation worthy of praise been prepared to forget his past and start afresh on a new road if he had been willing to play the game. I think he has realised a certain amount of his blunders and wishes to stage a come-back and try and make a fresh start, but his past follows him and his prejudices are deep set, and once he regains power he is bound to be vindictive. He is a man of exceptional patience and it is hard to evoke his anger in his present position. This ought to deter us, not to blind us and draw us into taking a responsibility on behalf of the Albanian people when the majority of them are, for all practical purposes, in a huge concentration camp where they can have no say in the matter and cannot voice their opinions. We have to be very careful and go slow as regards Albania's future internal régime. We have to think hard and objectively.

But to come back on the chronological trend of events. When he came to England his foolish young advisers wanted recognition at once and pronounced boldly that Zog was the legal Head of Albania, that he had a Government in exile, etc. etc. and naturally they were ignored by the British Government. It was a great mistake on their part to start shouting at a time when England was fighting for her very life and when Zog had been admitted here as a private individual on the promise that he would not participate in political activities.

The British Government had, unfortunately for us, recognised *de facto*, if not *de jure*, the annexation of Albania by Italy and had communicated to King Zog that they did not recognise him. But this could have been bypassed if tackled the right way at the right time as all contracts, undertakings and agreements are null and void in war with the enemy. I went to see him and told him plainly that in England he should change his ways of dealing with people. I advised him as to what he should do to regain some of his lost prestige as I thought my ten years in England had given me a better understanding of the English character and mentality. Others too advised him, both British and Albanians. But Zog took no advice, although he patiently listened to all one said. He thought he knew best. He had been led to believe that by his '*yes men*' in Albania.

When the Italo-Greek war was in progress in Albania we had another chance of voicing our claim to recognition as our people in Albania were fighting the Italians and were therefore materially helping the Allied cause. We begged of the King to play a more active part and make a public statement which we could have published. He was not inclined to do this but we put pressure upon him and eventually he agreed to something that was prepared on his behalf but he would not give it to the press here before, as he said, he had obtained the approval of the Foreign Office to do so. He is afraid of the press. It is quite understandable that the Foreign Office could not, under the circumstances prevailing at the time, pronounce themselves either way and so the draft is, I believe, somewhere in some file, but has not to this day seen public light.

I am told the King was asked to go to Greece and to Albania when certain parts of it were freed from the Italians, to try and rally the Albanian people to fight harder. I cannot vouch as to this because I have no proof myself. The King's story is that he asked to be permitted to go but was not allowed to do so as the Greeks did not wish it. In any case he said he could not go without promises from the British Government, and these promises were not forthcoming. I could have told him that.

When the Greeks, who fought the invader so valiantly, were advancing on Albanian soil they were at first joined and supported as friends by the Albanians, but they soon went back on their promises and, blinded by their temporary successes, rather liked bringing up old claims. As soon as Korça and Gjinokastra were liberated, the Greeks celebrated '*the return of the towns to their mother country*' (towns which were never theirs) and brought from Janina the Greek Bishop who was responsible for the massacres of 1913-14. When Himara was taken, the Greeks issued a Royal Proclamation annexing the territory. No wonder the Albanians only put half their heart in fighting on the Greek side. While fighting was going on, and Albanians were taking part, very little on their efforts was published in the press here or elsewhere. The Greeks managed to keep this news away from the world. The British people and press were thus misled into thinking the Albanians were Italianised. The British were naturally not inclined to intervene for the Greeks were their Allies and were at the height of their glory. They must be kept in the fight, and it was not politic, at that stage, to say anything about their unjust claims to someone else's territory. But I feel sure the Greeks were not promised any parts of Albania except, perhaps, that whatever claims they had would be '*sympathetically considered*', when the time came. In the meanwhile the Albanian question was kept pending. They had, and still have, numerous *'influential friends'*.

What is worse is that even now, when their own Government is in exile, they have laid claims to Southern Albania (which they wishfully call Northern Epirus) and have given publicity to their designs. We have tried hard to get our own view published and heard and considered. But our friends are few, we lack men, we lack funds, we still seem to lack unity abroad, and it is imperative we must hurry and do everything possible now, at once, to save our country. We must prepare our own case and must insist to be heard at the Peace Conference.

We have been given to believe that the situation as regards Albania's future is grave. Our friends who were supposed to be in *'the know'* of things first said that it was because of King Zog's claim to the Albanian throne; the widespread belief that the Albanians refused to accept him; the fact that he was in England, etc. etc. that were the main obstacles to Britain and the Allies giving recognition to Albania. We could not understand this point of view as we were not asking them to decide what the internal political set-up in Albania should be but that they declare, in principle, that they would guarantee the independence of the country after the war. That their belief must have been based on the above evidence, however, was quite clear, as in the summer of 1940 the Foreign Office spokesman in the House of Commons in answer to a question said that the British Government were sympathetic to the Albanian cause and they would consider *"collaborating with an association of persons representing the Albanian people"*.

This made it clearer than ever that they were not prepared to recognise, and work with, King Zog. The situation is still the same now. They do give facilities of a private nature to King Zog, and they have been considerate and hospitable to him in a private capacity, but as far as is known, in no way has the British Government officially treated with him in any political matter. They do not recognise him as the Legal Representative of Albania. And we are not surprised in the least. It was suggested to us once that if he signed some formal declaration renouncing his claim to the throne, we might be able to get better hearing for our case and perhaps gain recognition of Albania's independence after the war.

Later, however, the same source of friends advised us that it was really because of the Greek claims that Albania was not being mentioned in any way. It was believed the Greeks had used every influence to achieve their aim by at least leaving the question open to discussion. In this way we would not be represented at any of the Allied Conferences, and therefore could not, at the appropriate time oppose their claims. I believe, nevertheless, that very few people are deceived by the Greek claims and the propaganda supporting them. In a White Paper they have published they openly claimed Southern Albania.

It has been under such leaderless conditions, and unsupported by any official or unofficial body to take up our cause, that we have been working. The last Albanian Cabinet which left Albania with the King and reached Greece and Istanbul, for reasons not yet clear to us, was dispersed - some remaining in Greece, some in Turkey and the East and others returning to Albania and Italy. Of who they were and what they were I am not going to speak for I am certain you know them better than I do. But what is important is that notwithstanding suggestions made, advice given to and even pressure put on, King Zog, he never dissolved the Cabinet to form another which, as a body, we believe, irrespective of political events, would have gained a hearing and perhaps procured for us a chance to hold our own.

The people in Albania have continued to fight and to resist the Italians in every way, and I expect you have heard of their heroic exploits from the press and other sources. Albanian patriots, after the collapse of Greece, have, under their own leaders, joined the Yugoslav and Greek and Bulgarian guerrilla armies. Their efforts are quite well known even though little publicity has been given them and they have given the Axis forces more than a headache. But they expect, and are entitled to expect, that we, their free compatriots abroad, should make every effort and sacrifice to help them achieve the only purpose for which they are so bravely laying down their lives - to be rid of oppressors and invaders and assure for themselves and their children a better future. The Albanian people demand, and will continue to demand, that their rights should be respected.

Prompted by all these, Logoreci and I, and all the other Albanians here, have done all in our power to secure some promise for our country. We have approached friends, we have approached Committees, we have appealed in the press, we have approached Governments, but we have received no other satisfaction beyond sympathy. And we were not under any circumstances prepared to remain slaves because of King Zog's misrule. At least we could have a hard try in the hopes that there would, in the end, be found someone with a sufficient sense of justice to see that it was no use sacrificing a whole nation "*to appease enemies or propitiate allies*" as Miss Durham put it in a letter to the British press. Zog only got worried if the press attacked him or his immediate interests, but he did not seem to be alarmed if large portions of our country and our best towns were in danger of being given away.

May we be forgiven, but basing our fears on not so distant events, we even thought that it was not beyond him to negotiate with the Greeks and Yugoslavs if he could secure their support for his return to the Throne. We heard he saw Greek and Yugoslav Ministers in private and had long conversations with them and only told us that they had assured him that their respective countries had no designs on Albanian territory, the frontiers of which had already been delimited and recognised. And yet they, the Greeks especially, continued publicising their claims to Southern Albania as far as Valona and Pogradec! The situation was getting desperate.

There is here a certain organisation called *'The Balkan Committee'*. I do not know if you ever heard of them. As the name implies it is composed of people with knowledge of, and interest in, the Balkans. Miss Durham, General Percy,[56] Mrs. Herbert and a few other friends of Albania are members of this Committee. Among its members are Members of the House of Lords and M.P.s, and private individuals of all walks of life, but because of the war not all members have been meeting regularly. The President of this Committee is Lord Noel Buxton[57], and the active Chairman is Sir Edward Boyle, Bt. The latter has quite a good knowledge of Yugoslavia, Bulgaria, Greece and of Albania. He has not been to Albania for any length of time but has visited it on several occasions since the beginning of the century and has always kept in touch with Albanian matters. We count him as one of our active friends, and as he is a personal friend of mine I had continually appealed to him to try and use his social standing and influence and his knowledge of Balkan affairs to help us to obtain justice. He personally, and through Lord Cecil and others, tried to get the situation cleared but, in the past, authoritative friends have not encouraged him to raise the question in the House in order not to bring the matter to a head. It might embarrass the Government and it might also evoke an unfavourable reply from them.

Last March Sir Edward asked me to prepare a short memorandum on Albania. He wanted a statement representing the agreed opinion of the Albanians here, which the Committee could discuss and consider. This I did in co-operation with Logoreci and Zavalani. The idea was, we were told, that this memorandum of ours should, after recommendation by the Committee, be submitted to the Foreign Office and the State Department in Washington, when the right moment came. I do not know if any other reasons urged Sir Edward to ask for this statement at this particular moment besides our appeals at various times. The request was so urgently presented that I had no time to ask your advice on the matter then. After the meeting of the Committee, when I read the statement, I handed it to Sir Edward for circulation to, and comments from, those members of the Committee who were close friends of Albania. These were Miss Durham, Mrs. Herbert, General Percy and Sir Robert Hodgson[58] (former Minister to Albania).

In the meantime the news got into the papers in the wrong light, as you will see from enclosures. It did not represent the truth of the matter at all and I wrote and denied it. But Zog was alarmed and his Minister of Court, Sotir Martini, put sand in the wheels by writing to Sir Edward defending Zog's case without first consulting us of what was said at the Committee. But as they trust no one they would not have believed us anyway. Correspondence followed between everyone, and I kept in touch with Sir Edward, General

Percy, Miss Durham and Sir Robert. The question became complicated and the issue was enlarged.

In the memorandum, after discussion and disagreement with Zavalani who, to our astonishment, upheld Çekrezi as leader, we decided to suggest the formation of an Albanian National Committee with, say, Bishop Noli as its Chief, as this had also been apparently agreed by a meeting of Albanians in Paris. Logoreci and I agreed to implement this by putting your name forward as well. We did not know if there was any chance at all of Bishop Noli or you accepting the office. But we became suspicious of Çekrezi's work as Zavalani was, even after our memorandum, trying to get recognition for Çekrezi and his organisation. He was in somewhat of a hurry to do so. We did not know then that he had already arranged with Çekrezi and had been appointed as his London representative.

I then cabled you for information on the 1st of April. I was ever so glad to receive from you such a detailed and early reply. Mainly because of the second question in your cable I thought it advisable to consult Sir Edward Boyle, General Percy and Miss Durham, as I cabled you on the 8th April. This entailed more correspondence between us and between members of the Committee and further delay to my answering you.

Martini continued to write to Sir Edward in fear of the King being left out of any combination. In view of what had transpired I did not think it right to advise the King of your cabled proposal, but in an interview I had with him later, I mentioned what you had said of Çekrezi and that you were collaborating with Bishop Noli. He was quick to say that you were a friend of his and that although you had criticised him severely he was going to write to you. He informed me he had read of a proposal you were supposed to have made in the '*Dielli*' and I gathered it was the same as the one in your cable to me, but as I do not receive the '*Dielli*' I was ignorant of the fact.

He said you had left the door open for collaboration. When I asked why he had not kept in touch with you, he said you had asked him for $28,000 and he had not sent you the money as it was too much! At the same interview when I mentioned Bishop Noli as an important personality to be considered and consulted, that he was Head of the Albanian Church in U.S.A. and of international reputation, and that you two were the strongest elements in the Albanian national scheme of the strongest Albanian colony, he told me, in confidence, that he had written to Bishop Noli but that Noli had replied that nothing useful could be done in the matter unless the British Government had given us recognition. Of course I was not in a position to know how the proposal had been put to Noli. Perhaps Zog had asked him to be his Prime Minister, and without any guarantee on Zog's part, to work Zog's schemes and condone his past? No wonder Noli had not agreed to collaborate with him.

But of one thing I am convinced, that King Zog does not want any form of Committee of Albanians, which might get recognition, to be formed unless he forms it or unless he is first recognised by the Allied Governments as the sole legal representative of Albania. He is afraid lest such a Committee might be strong enough to negotiate with him as to what is to be done, after Albania has been liberated, in the way of internal régime.

Our contention is that as a majority of people in Albania are believed to be against him and fear a repetition of his 15 years' rule, and as most of those people are the ones who now lead the fight against the Italians, it is important that if he were to be accepted and confirmed as our leader, the King should sign a formal declaration plainly laying down that the future political organisation of the country is to be left to a freely elected Constituent Assembly to decide and that he will abide by their decision. This implies that he will only return to the Albanian throne if the people thus confirm him. I do not think he is prepared to do this, which shows that he does not enjoy the trust of his people.

From copies of correspondence which I will send you, you will see that we have made this quite plain to those English friends who are trying to help us. They have told us that our only chance is in unity and have advised that we accept Zog as a figure-head for the duration at least and that he would be a good spearhead. We have told them that, with all due respect to everyone, we would not like to take the responsibility of presenting the

61Albanian people with a *fait accompli*.

On the Balkan Committee having studied the question from more than one angle called a meeting at the Dorchester Hotel to which we were invited to hear their recommendations, which the Chairman said they had agreed upon after very long correspondence between themselves and after much deliberation. Logoreci, Zavalani and I were present as the original trio who started the Albanian case going. At this special meeting King Zog had seen to it that his special people with his instructions were present too.

These were Mr. Kerran[59], a German naturalised British subject who acts as Zog's agent, in the capacity of solicitor, for his private and certain official matters, and Mr. Qazim Kastrati[60] about whom please see biographical note. As an Englishman Mr. Kerran had found his way to the Committee before we, the Albanians, were called in, and had taken part in the deliberations - a thing we did not approve of as he was bound to be one-sided. We therefore felt that we were to receive the verdict from a jury not all of whom enjoyed our confidence and respect. Of him more in the enclosures, as I protested to Sir Edward Boyle[61] in a letter I addressed to him later on.

It was not that we were against King Zog unreasonably, but we wanted the Committee to formulate an unbiased opinion and then perhaps, from our evidence and from whatever material they had studied, which was not available to us as it might have been of a confidential nature, they might, with a clear conscience and conviction, advise us of the best course to follow. There was some heated argument and frank expression of views at this meeting when the Chairman read the Committee's recommendations to us. Logoreci, Zavalani and I left them under no doubt as to our opinion.

There seemed two distinct camps among the witnesses, one composed of us three who wanted more guarantees from Zog before we agreed to anything, and the other composed of Kerran and Kastrati supporting unconditional acceptance of Zog. Of course, Zog must have had a full report from the latter two that very night, and I expect three of his subjects are in his bad books!

The Committee heard our views, answered a few questions and made a few remarks, but altered nothing very much from their original draft of recommendations except under Clause 3 regarding Zog's undertaking which you will see from the enclosed copy of letter from Sir Edward Boyle to Mr. Sotir Martini[62]. You will note that this letter was written to Martini for Zog and Sir Edward kindly sent me a copy confidentially. It has not been published, it is not common knowledge yet, and is not for publication. I have not yet heard of the result or of Zog's reply, nor whether General Percy and Sir Robert Hodgson have seen him. They were to see him on behalf of the Committee in order to discuss the matter with him and enlighten him.

When I last saw the General I made it plain to him that the formal undertaking required by us from Zog should be drafted in such a way as to be acceptable by all 'reasonable Albanians'. We would not agree to just any promise through Martini.

That is where the question stands today. I also asked the Committee to get in touch with Bishop Noli and yourself and get your views on the subject. I do not know if they have done this, but Sir Edward said at the meeting that he was going to communicate the Committee's recommendations to me and that I should communicate them to you. That is how it would have been had Martini not written again to the Committee on behalf of King Zog. If King Zog does not accept the recommendations, we have to think out another solution and Bishop Noli and yourself must take the lead. We have been given to understand plainly that only from your side, representing the largest colony, something might be achieved through the State Dept. at Washington. Miss Durham has advised me that she is also writing to you.

Before I close I have one more comment to make and that is on the last clause of the Committee's recommendations: the Mandate question. Personally, and without prejudice of any kind, I think, under the circumstances, the idea would probably be a good one. I know I say this at the risk of being called unpatriotic, but I think I have a fairly good idea of the conditions of my country and of my countrymen. This might be the best way, for a time, to save us from ourselves and our neighbours. At least the people who under Zog's régime have gone without the bare necessities of life - of even such a primary commodity as salt - could have a better lot in life. On the other hand I have pointed out - and Logoreci much more strongly so - that it is impolite to bring the question up at the present moment because of Balkan jackals. They might perpetrate that we are incapable of governing ourselves.

Some of my more intimate friends and members of the Committee have told me that of course as we ourselves under these recommendations would ask for the Mandate of our own free will, we could by an agreement terminate it whenever we thought we had been well stabilised and capable of running our own house safely and efficiently. They believe that it would be a great blessing to Albania as an important factor of development and organisation of our own latest capacities.

I shall keep you informed of any later developments, but in the meantime we would all be grateful for Bishop Noli's and your observations and comments. A reply from Bishop Noli and yourself, believe me, will have our utmost consideration and respect. It would be a lead from patriots and veterans which is bound to be followed by one and all as an impartial advice for the good of our country.

With best wishes,
Yours sincerely,

Dervish Duma

CAS. D.D. archive

[44] 24th June, 1942

Dervish Duma to Faik Konitza

Dear Mr. Konitza,

After I had mailed my letter of 12th June to you, I received a letter from Sir Edward Boyle asking me whether it would be best for the Balkan Committee, as such, to communicate their recommendations to Bishop Noli and yourself - and even to Chekrezi - direct.

Logoreci and I, in concert with our friends, have agreed to this, as we, ourselves, had suggested this course to Sir Edward in a letter I wrote to him some weeks ago. I think it is better so, as in this way you will all know positively that the recommendations are impartial and authentic from the Committee. You will thus have an opportunity to comment on their recommendations and give your views directly to the Committee without any intermediaries, although Sir Edward thinks that I should still act as a Liaison Officer between our English friends and the Albanian centres in U.S.A.

I believe Sir Edward will not get in touch with you, however, before he has received a satisfactory reply from King Zog, and before he has had a report from Sir Robert Hodgson and General Percy on their interview with the King and their opinion on him and his views.

Sir Edward further adds in his letter to me that I should not send anything to America yet until I hear further from him. It looks as if a hitch may have occurred somewhere, or that the Committee may not have received a favourable reply from Zog - or that, perhaps they may have changed their minds as to their original recommendations.

Nevertheless, the case being as it is, as I have already sent you copy of their recommendations, I would be very grateful to you, indeed, if you would be so kind as to treat my letter and all enclosures as strictly private and confidential until you hear from Sir Edward Boyle, on behalf of the

Committee, direct. I think this is bound to be very soon now as I have seen General Percy who was going to have a meeting with Sir Edward and Sir Robert this week.

I understand that Zavalani wrote to Bishop Noli a month or so ago and he says that in reply Noli has informed him that he (Noli) cannot take active part because he is now a naturalised American subject, but would be glad to help us in an advisory capacity. I would be glad to know if this is so and if you think there is any possibility of him changing his mind and collaborating with you actively.

Do you think that, notwithstanding their mentality and policy, Chekrezi's crowd could be induced to take part in a United Front? In your view, would any useful purpose be served by including them? The idea here among ourselves and our friends, is that it is absolutely necessary for a United Front to include, as far as possible, all Albanians irrespective of their views on internal politics in view of the outside threats to our country's future independence. When together, ideas could be thrashed out by their respective Leaders in Committee and a *'modus vivendi'* could be found. I am sure all Albanians would welcome a finished article, so to speak, moulded and presented by leaders like Noli and yourself in whom they have great faith and trust. With a united voice the State Department in Washington and the Foreign Office could then be approached boldly.

It is an inexplicable phenomenon but Sir Edward tells me that Zog (if Martini's letters to Sir Edward could be taken to convey Zog's instructions, as I think they do) does not seem to be willing to give even a promise in writing for free elections in Albania, after the country has been liberated, so that a Constituent Assembly, representative of the people could determine Albania's future regime. This, I think, is a very serious implication, for he thus takes the attitude that as he contends to be still legally Sovereign Head of Albania, he has the right to impose his will on the people: - an act which the people cannot be expected to, and will not, tolerate. Having lost his prestige, to show goodwill now is essential.

However, we shall soon know what the outcome of our endeavours on this side of the Atlantic will be, and I will write to you again in greater length of the future developments.

Dervish Duma

CAS. D.D. archive

[45] August 21, 1942

To Dervish Duma
1530 Sixteenth Street
Washington, D.C.

Dear Mr. Duma,

I have received in due time both your letters dated respectively 12th and 24th of June, 1942. I wish to thank you for the pains you took to send me all that valuable information. My answer is overdue, but the reason for the delay is that I wished to finish a journey through the Albanian communities here before writing to you.

I quite agree with you on the danger involved in having as a leader a man who eventually may think it in his interest to give up a part of Albania in order to secure the rest for himself. However, Noli thinks, we have to take a chance since Zog happens to symbolise the unity and independence of Albania, and anyhow we shall be able to contradict him if at the last moment he should deviate from the right path.

As I told you in one of my cables, Vatra ignored Chekrezi's so-called *'congress'*. But Noli insisted that afterwards a delegation of Vatra and a delegation of the *'congress'* headed by Chekrezi himself should meet in order to discuss the terms of a united front. I was not present, but advised Vatra to follow Noli's lead. So the two delegations met with Noli and Chekrezi present. Chekrezi started an irrelevant and bombastic speech that lasted one hour and a half and was frequently interrupted by cries of *"You are insane!"* and *"You are a Greco-Serb paid agent!"* and *"Go and drown yourself!"*. Noli and others retorted with brief speeches that finally drove Chekrezi out of the meeting (which had taken place in the Albanian Cathedral of St. George). Chekrezi went out abundantly perspiring and muttering absurd threats.

Noli was of the opinion that Chekrezi should not be attacked in the *'Dielli'* for one full month, and I consented to this arrangement. The idea was to give Chekrezi the opportunity to think matters over, but he immediately started attacking Noli in his paper. As a sequel to this meeting a great many followers of Chekrezi left his alleged *'organisation'*. Moreover, previously, Chekrezi was hooted in Chicago, nine-tenths of the people present leaving the hall before he had finished his talk. At other places similar incidents have taken place. It appears that Chekrezi's hope is to be recognized as the head of the Albanian State in exile and thereby get funds available to the United Nations from the Lend-Lease Bill: a most laughable hope, because, uninformed though the United States may be about Albania, it is not simple-minded enough to fall victim to an adventurer.

Tajar Zavalani, whose description by you is quite interesting and fits the information I had gathered from other sources, is not, however, to be blamed for Chekrezi's misrepresentation of the reasons which made B.B.C. withdraw their invitation to Miss Durham to make a broadcast on Albania. I happen to know, from a confession made to Bishop Noli by Chekrezi's assistant editor, that Zavalani's letter on Miss Durham's intended broadcast did not contain one word about King Zog: the fanciful addition was entirely Chekrezi's and the assistant editor protested against this way of handling the correspondence.

The long letter I received from King Zog was quite reasonable and intelligently written. In my answer to him, I suggested the immediate formation of a small cabinet drawn from Albanians living in England; and in another letter to Mr. Martini I strongly suggested that you and Mr. Logoreci should be by all means induced to take part in the new patriotic undertaking. I warned Mr. Martini of the danger of upsetting all the work so far done if King Zog again indulged in his old game of forgetting pledges that he had voluntarily given.

I had a big laugh at the conversation between King Zog and you, which you report in your letter. It is false that I asked Zog for twenty-eight thousand dollars; I only told him, at his request, that the over-due credits of this former Legation were eight thousand dollars, which he consented to pay immediately and never did. It is equally false that he has been in correspondence with Noli. As a matter of fact, when Noli found out that identical cables to the one he had received from Zog had been sent also to twenty or thirty other persons here, he decided not even to answer. Noli's fundamental idea is that Chekrezi, as a Greco-Serb agent, is apt to do a good deal of harm to Albania; while, as an uncouth man who never washes and disturbs everybody with his bodily odours, he is casting ridicule on Albania. The Bishop thinks Zog, although by no means a good, let alone an ideal, leader, is protected by his position and experience and would put an end to the intrigues of Chekrezi and other similar adventurers who may spring up in these troubled times.

I now close my letter, but will write you soon again because I have left out some points that require elucidation.

Please give my regards to Mr. Anton Logoreci, and believe me,

Yours sincerely,

Faik Konitza

CAS. D.D. archive

[46] 4th September 1942

To Faik Konitza
The Old House,
West Horsley,
Surrey.

Dear Mr. Konitza,

I hope you have received my air-mailed letters of 12th and 24th June last. I would very much appreciate a word from you as we are all looking towards Mgr. Fan Noli and yourself for leadership.

Mr. Peter Kolonia has kindly sent me copies of *'Dielli'* (15th and 29th July 1942) and I have learned of the renewed efforts of Mgr. Noli and yourself, and of the members of VATRA to bring about a United Front. I have every hope you will succeed for it seems to be the only right way. I feel certain all Albanians in U.S.A. will follow suit. I have written to Mr. Kolonja[63] and, as Secretary of the Board of Vatra, I feel sure he will bring my letter to your notice.

As soon as I received Mr. Hulusi's[64] cable of 6th July conveying Vatra's unanimous resolution for a United Front I circulated the appeal to all Albanians here and cabled Vatra accordingly. At several meetings we had in London afterwards we discussed the question and embodied a few suggestions in a cable we sent to Vatra on the 26th July. These were only our suggestions, but you could see from the signatures that none of the King's staff signed although two of them took part in our discussions and were in agreement with us. I am afraid the King does not seem to tolerate, much, any suggestions or constructive criticism, and his *'Scribes'* will, naturally, do nothing which is not to his liking.

The King seems to think that one should either be with him totally, whether he is right or wrong, or against him. He does not seem to appreciate, however, that one may not agree with him in all he says or does, but that, yet, one can, when it may be in the interests of the country, try and collaborate with him and that a critical element is healthy to the cause. Anyhow he has not kept the Albanians in London informed of his activities - as he trusts no one - when all the Albanians are working for the same cause.

Perhaps we are wrong, but we think there should be nothing concerning Albania which he should hide from those who are endeavouring to promote the cause of Albania. For example, the cable he is supposed to have addressed to *'all Albanians abroad'* on the 7th of April was not shown to us until we heard about it casually and demanded to see it. When an undated copy was given us on the 17th of July we did not know when or to whom it had been sent. We are waiting to hear the results of Vatra's efforts.

Since I last wrote to you, you will, no doubt, have also heard from Sir Edward Boyle and will have received the Balkan Committee's recommendations of which Mr. Chekrezi seems to have made so much fuss in Liria. Having received Mgr. Noli's cable and a letter from Chekrezi, Sir Edward wrote to them both and he was kind enough to let me see the letters. I enclose copy of a private letter Sir Edward wrote to me on this occasion, which I think you might like to see.

No doubt Mgr. Noli will have shown you Sir Edward's letter to him, and copy of a letter Sir Edward wrote to Sotir Martini regarding the same matter. I hope the controversy has now been settled and they will deal with more serious business. Chekrezi is beyond understanding, and I am afraid is doing a lot of harm. By keeping the Albanians apart he is in fact playing the same game as Zog wants to play but with a different purpose and different results. Whereas he is irresponsible furthering other people's ends, even though unintentionally, by shouting publicly, King Zog is doing it behind the scenes with selfishness as the motive.

I hope you have received copies of a reprint from the *'Contemporary Review'* of Logoreci's article on Albania, which we sent you. This will make the Greek claims on Albania quite plain. I now enclose a short memorandum showing what the Yugoslavs think of Albania's future. It is an English observer's account of what took place at the meeting where Capt. Vandeleur Robinson[65] spoke on Albania. It does not deal with Capt. Robinson's talk which was on the same lines as his book *'Albania's Road to Freedom'* and which was quite friendly to the Albanian cause. It just deals with the more important point which arose in the discussions: the Jugoslav point of view as expressed by Milan Gavrilovic, Minister of Justice in the Jugoslav Government in London.

This may perhaps; explain Chekrezi's attitude at the meeting with representatives of the Vatra when he declared that he had been *'advised'* by the Greek and Jugoslav representatives in Washington not to join in a United Front if this included King Zog. The reasons for this excuse not to join, and prevent, a United Front might now with ample reason be traced elsewhere and that King Zog is just a perfect excuse. I wonder what other excuse Chekrezi would find if King Zog were left out of the provisional arrangement? I suppose he would want to be Chairman of the movement with his policy unopposed!

If I may say so, I think both *'Dielli'* and *'Liria'* should now concern themselves much more with these claims, which seem to hamper Albania's recognition of independence instead of with trifles and misunderstandings among Albanians - even if a United Front were not achieved there should be agreement on this.

A strong appeal from Bishop Noli and yourself on these matters should stir our papers in America to greater action in defence of our country's just cause. Even if it were found necessary to neutralise King Zog and Chekrezi, I daresay you should get good results. To be so inactive in matters threatening our liberty at the moment is dangerous as it may lead to the end finding us in the same position as we are today with no strong body voicing our rights.

Miss Durham had kindly shown me her letter to you and I was glad you gave it publication in *'Dielli'*. The Albanians, as you rightly infer, could not afford to be deaf to her call for she has devoted a great part of her life to help Albania - as you know better than any one else - and I hope they will respond to it. Events are proving how right she is.

Please forgive me for worrying you with these matters, but besides Bishop Noli and yourself I know of no greater patriots in America to whom I could write thus and not be misunderstood.

With deepest respect and highest regards to Mgr. Noli and yourself, and wishing you the best of luck, I remain

Yours sincerely,

D. Duma

CAS. D.D. archive

[47] 26 November 1942

translated by Peter Rennie

To Sotir Martini

My dear Mr.Martini,

I do not understand why you have sent by ordinary post, instead of by air, your letter of 27 September 1942, which has taken exactly a month to arrive here.

Regarding the increasing cost of living here, the 400 dollars a month are a little insufficient; but if you can not do better, that's all right.

You say "*200 or 300 dollars a month*" for Bishop Noli. I beg you to choose the 300 rather than the 200. The Bishop arrived the other day from Boston, and has read your letter. He approved of it in general.

The treasurer and effective chief of '*Vatra*' is Mr. Vasil Pani; consequently you should send him the 600 dollars for '*Dielli*'.

Your idea of 100 dollars a month for an official as press secretary is good. You can therefore send me this sum to dispose of, as for the rest you can send me, if you prefer, all the above mentioned sums, which I shall forward to the recipients as received.

I remain yours devotedly,

Faik Konitza

SSEES Naçi Collection 3/4

[48] 5 November 1942

translated by Peter Rennie

To Sotir Martini

Dear Minister,

I have received your letter of 27 September 1942 and have the honour of informing you that I accept the post of the King's representative in Washington.

It would be necessary for His Majesty to send a letter to the Ambassador of the United States in London, begging him to transmit its contents to Washington. In this letter he should say that the painful exception made of Albania by not recognising officially the government in exile, even after the entry of Italy into the war, renders superfluous the despatch of an official Minister to Washington; on the other hand, as it will become more and more evident that Albania could play in the near future a useful role in the Allied cause, the King has considered naming as his personal representative in Washington Faik Konitza who has been the Albanian envoy to the United States from 1925 to 1939.

Something similar will suffice, I think, to establish my position as a non-offical representative.

Be pleased to accept the assurance of my high regards,

Faik Konitza

SSEES Naçi Collection 3/4

[49] July 1942

translated by Peter Rennie

To Sotir Martini

Representative of HM King Zog,
1530 Sixteenth Street,
Washington DC

Sir,

Your letter of 17 August 1942 has only just arrived. Tajar Zavalani has not yet come here; but if he comes, he will find matters quite different from those which Koste Chekrezi had told him.

Meanwhile I have received your radiogram of 16 September announcing the imminent arrival of the King's delegate. I hope that he will not be too delayed so that we can at last get to work.

Yours devotedly,

Faik Konitza

SSEES Naçi Collection 3/4

[50] 2 October 1942

translated by Peter Rennie

To His Excellency, Mr. Sotir Martini,
Minister Plenipotentiary

Dear Minister,

I received, a few days ago, the second delivery of a thousand dollars. They arrived just in time because I have still some communities to visit. I leave tomorrow.

The spirit in the Albanian communities here is generally favourable. They laugh at Chekrezi, who passes the time drinking and shouting, but who has nothing substantial. His so-called *'partisans'* are only grecophiles who have never loved Albania. Chekrezi's aim is to become recognised as the head of '*Free Albania*' and thus to draw at his pleasure from the funds of the '*Lend-Lease Bill*'; the chimera of an ignorant adventurer.

The Albanians here wonder why the King has not yet formed an Albanian cabinet in exile. This measure would put an end to Chekrezi's machinations. But perhaps you have reasons for this delay of which we are ignorant.

I remain yours devotedly,

Faik Konitza

(This is a copy of a letter which has already been sent to you a week ago)

SSEES Naçi Collection 3/4

[51] 3 September 1942

translated by Peter Rennie

To His Majesty King Zog

(Copy of a telegram sent to Your Majesty, 20 July 1942)

After conversations we have agreed to submit to Your Majesty following suggestions Stop Important to form immediately small cabinet with members from among Albanians living in England preferably knowing English Stop Necessary without delay to name representative in Washington and one in London Stop Necessary finally to send here a trustworthy person as your delegate to discuss certain points Stop Sending someone from here impossible Stop Details follow in letter to Your Majesty Stop

Faik Konitza

SSEES Naçi Collection 3/4

[52] 24 July 1942

translated by Peter Rennie

To His Excellency Mr. Sotir Martini

Sir,

Koste Chekrezi was boasting that the diplomatic representatives of Albania in Cairo and Ankara were his agents. He no longer does it, but he has not denied it.

It would be important to teach him a lesson. If Mr. Abdul Sula and Djadjuli each wrote me a short letter in French denouncing Chekrezi's fantasies, I would take this opportunity to inform the American Government of this matter. But we must make haste.

I remain Sir, your devoted
Faik Konitza

SSEES Naçi Collection 3/4

[53] September 1942

translated by Peter Rennie

To His Excellency, Mr. Sotir Martini

Dear Mr. Martini,

I have received your delivery of a thousand dollars as well as your radiograms and diverse communications.

I had already arranged, by phone and letters, the progress of our organisation. On arrival in Boston, I immediately began final conversations, the results of which have been communicated without delay to the King by telegram and letter. Copies of the letter and of the telegram will shortly be sent in case the originals will have been lost.

The organisation of our movement with King Zog at its head will be successful in spite of the powerless opposition of Chekrezi, whose absurd dream is to have himself recognised as Head of Free Albania and thus benefit from loans of American money under the *'Lend-Lease Bill'*. Noli's idea to invite Chekrezi to join us was really to give proof that Chekrezi did not wish to join, which is now abundantly clear.

There is only one fault which could abort our movement; this would be if the King were to undertake engagements and then not pursue them. You know that HM unfortunately has this habit. Remember his action regarding me. For the last three years I have lived on loans, and my old loans have not yet been paid. I leave all this to your judgment.

Bishop Noli ought to have received a gift of several thousand dollars to shelter him from the capriciousness of the crowd which could force him tomorrow to behave differently from now. The gift ought to have been made discreetly with a letter from the King telling him that the sum is for the Bishop's private charities.

Then there is the question of Mr.Vasil J. Pani, a kindhearted businessman who, with one or two friends, gave about five thousand dollars to *'Vatra'*. In sending a personal cheque to Mr. Pani, the King would perform an act of justice which would wipe out the past.

Finally, I think you ought to recruit Dervish Duma and Anton Logoreci into our movement. I know them and I shall answer for them if they are well treated. You have had perhaps complaints from them, but the present situation requires a conciliatory spirit.

This is what I have to say to you for the moment. Do as you wish.

I remain yours devotedly,

Faik Konitza

SSEES Naçi Collection 3/4

[54] August 1942

translated by Peter Rennie

To His Majesty King Zog

Copy of a letter sent to Your Majesty ten days ago

received 10.8.42

Sire,

Following Your Majesty's instructions, I have quickly held negotiations with my Albanian political friends, and we have concluded an agreement, the principal points of which I have submitted to you by telegraph. I repeat them here in more detail.

We are of the opinion that the Cabinet ought to be constituted without delay, as Your Majesty has suggested ...

Finally, we believe that in view of the difficulty of communications, these ministers should be chosen from among the Albanians who are already in England. It would be possible when the period of peace negotiations approaches to replace the ministers that Your Majesty nominates now by Albanian personalities whose work would be more effective.

It would be desirable for Your Majesty to have a representative in Washington and another in London; but to avoid the title of minister, which would place these officials in an embarrassing position so long as Your government has not been officially recognised. The title of representative, on the other hand, is simple, flexible and lends itself to all occasions.Later we shall form here a Council of capable persons to assist the movement and who will not receive any remuneration.

The expenses in America, in our opinion, will amount to around $5,000 (five thousand dollars) a month once the organisation is completed and operating. For the moment, the expenses will be more modest. They consist of the following:

1) The appointments and diverse expenses of Your representative in Washington, the amount being determined by Your Majesty
2) a subsidy of $600 (six hundred dollars) a month to *'Dielli'* to allow it to appear once a week
3) $400 (four hundred dollars) a month for the appointment and expenses of two permanent lecturers who will constantly visit the communities here and speak for the cause
4) $100 (one hundred dollars) a month for a press officer, an indispensible post here.

Finally, it would be good if Your Majesty were to send a trustworthy person here to make contact with us and to see things closely. We find it impossible to send someone from here.

If these suggestions please Your Majesty, the successful advance of the organisation would be better assured if an Anglo-American bank had charge of the payments on a basis that would avoid delays.

Albanian public opinion now has become favourable to Your Majesty; and this is due mainly to the eloquent work and influence of Monsignor Noli, who has succeeded in isolating Chekrezi. I thought for a moment that Mgr. Noli would be the ideal man for Prime Minister, but unfortunately the fact that he is now a United States citizen renders this choice difficult. But he will always be an able and vigilant adviser.

I am, Sire, Your obedient servant

Faik Konitza

SSEES Naçi Collection 3/4

[55] 24 July 1942

Legation of Switzerland
Washington D.C.
Attention: Mr. De Bourg
Italo-Albanian Affairs Division

The Last Hours of Konitza

On advice of the State Department, and following our telephone conversation of yesterday, I wish to advise you in writing of the death of Faik Konitza, Former Minister of Albania to the United States, on Tuesday, the fifteenth of December, 1942.

Mr. Konitza had suffered a stroke on Monday some time before five o'clock, for that is the time that Hattie Williams, a colored maid who had done his work for over fifteen years, found him lying on the bathroom floor. Mr. Konitza asked for me and I arrived at five-thirty o'clock. Mr. Konitza asked that I call Dr. Robert Oden, his physician and great friend. I did, and the doctor came shortly thereafter. He confirmed my fear that Mr. Konitza was dangerously ill, and said he would arrange for a nurse and/or hospital.

I remained with Mr. Konitza, and notified the resident manager of the apartment that I would remain until he was moved to a hospital. The resident manager, Mrs. Dyer, brought me a blanket and sat with me for a while. Mr. Konitza called me at nine twenty-five and again at nine fifty o'clock. The last time he called was to ask for water, but I asked him to wait. He seemed satisfied and turned over. This is the last time I talked to him, I had started a letter to my husband, who is now in the Army Air Force, and had made notes of events and time. My last note is 11:45. Faik Bey still labored breathing but seems OK. I'm going to pile up on the sofa and try to rest." About five o'clock on Tuesday I awoke and looked in the bedroom. He seemed to be sleeping peacefully and I was relieved that he was resting. I dozed off again and about eight o'clock I went in to see how he was. He had not moved. I walked around to the end of the bed and guessed the truth: his eyes were slightly open but dull. I called Dr. Oden, who told me to go pick up Mr. Konitza's hand. I did and reported that it was cold and firm. Dr. Oden said he would be over as soon as he was through with an operation.

Dr. Oden asked about Mr. Konitza's family - did I know where they were? Also he asked about his finances, for someone would have to guarantee the undertaker. I advised him that Mr. Konitza had fifteen dollars and fifty-four cents in the apartment, and I felt that was about all. I told him about the twenty-one hundred dollars that Sotir Martini, King Zog's Minister, had cabled. Pending settlement, Dr. Oden said he would guarantee the undertaker, and Hysong's was called.

I called the State Department and talked to Mr. Jones, of the Southeastern European Division. He advised me to call the Riggs Bank regarding the money, which I did. I talked to Mr. Dejunier (I'm not certain of that spelling), who advised me to cable Mr. Martini that Mr. Konitza was dead, and request him to instruct the Bank to pay me the funds to cover funeral and office expenses. This I did, paying seven dollars and ninety-two cents ($7.92) for it. I have had no answer as yet.

I notified Bishop Fan S. Noli in Boston, Massachusetts, and asked that he notify the Pan-Albanian Federation of America, *'Vatra'*. The Vatra, through an undertaker in Boston, Watterman, made arrangements with Hysong's to have Mr. Konitza's body shipped to Boston, where I understand the funeral will be held tomorrow, Sunday.

Regarding Mr. Konitza's assets: I would list first his library of perhaps two thousand five hundred books. I know it to be valuable, and that many of the books are rare. Father Cartwright, of the Immaculate Conception Church here in Washington, who was a great friend of Mr. Konitza's, knows something of the value of the library. However, I feel that this library must not be considered as something that can be sold: many times Mr. Konitza has told me that he wanted it to be part of the Albanian National Library. Somehow or other this wish must be carried out, the books could be catalogued and stored for the duration.

There are also some pictures and statuettes of undetermined value: two statuettes in original clay and seven water colors by the great Rodin. The apartment furnishings (living-room and bed-room furniture) were bought at Mayer & Company in 1940 for $487.35.

There are vases and utensils in copper, bronze, and silver, and a miscellaneous collection of kitchen equipment. I could not attempt to give an estimate of their value, but feel that it is not great. There is a Shaw-Walker file case and a steel wardrobe. Also there is a record player and an extensive collection of records.

In Mr. Konitza's personal things there are perhaps ten suits, and an undetermined number of top coats, hats, shoes, etc. There is a very fine collection of formal clothes. Mr. Konitza's personal wardrobe was ample. Mr. Konitza had no use for jewelry, and left very little. There is a watch, a ring with bloodstone setting, a stick-pin with the Albanian eagle design, and various cuff-links.

There is a miscellaneous collection of Albanian coins, medals, and seals. I believe them to be of little value, with the exception of one coin: it is a gold coin one and three-eighths inches in diameter, on one side of which is the Albanian eagle and the letters Fr. A, the number "100" and the date 1928. On the other side is a likeness of King Zog, and the inscription "Zog V - Alban - Rex." Aside from the value of the gold - or the actual money it represents - I believe it has added interest: I believe Mr. Konitza told me it was the first coin of its kind minted, and thus has perhaps an added value as a collector's item.

The above, with some property in Cook's possession in England, represents Mr. Konitza's assets, I believe. There is somewhere a gold cigarette case of quite some value, but I am of the opinion that it has been used to guarantee a loan. Mr. Shkemb Gura, an Albanian and good friend of Mr. Konitza's, knows of this matter, I believe.

As to debts, there is first the current month's rent on Mr. Konitza's apartment, No. 202, The Hightowers, 1530 16th Street, N. W. There are bills or telegrams, telephone, laundry, stationery, dentist; salaries are due his secretary, and the couple (colored) who have done his work in the apartment. I am of the opinion that Mr. Konitza had borrowed money from several friends, and these loans are still outstanding. I believe all these debts to amount to less than a thousand dollars. If necessary, I can furnish an itemized list of names and amounts I believe owing.

You asked for a comprehensive report, and I believe this letter is that.

Yours sincerely,

Charlotte A. Graham
Secretary to the Former Minister of Albania,
Faik Konitza

SSEES Naçi Collection 3/4t

[56] December 22, 1942

Letter to Sotir Martini

Dear Mr. Minister,

In my cable to you on the 16th of this month, I informed you that Faik Bey Konitza passed away on the previous day. He had called for me (I have acted as his secretary for nearly twelve years, and have been his friend for more years yet) and I arrived at his apartment about half past five o'clock. For the rest, rather than repeat, I refer you to my report to the Legation of Switzerland (copy of which is attached).

Funeral services were held for Faik Bey in Boston on Sunday, and I expect a full report will be made you by Bishop Noli and/or the Vatra.In the cable I advised you that your payment of twenty one hundred dollars to Faik Bey had not been effected. I sent this cable on the advice of the Riggs National Bank, but as yet I have had no answer. In the meantime, the Vatra guaranteed funeral expenses, and today I am in receipt of a letter advising me that two representatives will call tomorrow to talk with me: their names are Mr. Peter Tyko and Mr. Shefqet Bencha.

Faik Bey left some outstanding bills and had borrowed various sums from friends, pending the arrival of money from His Majesty. The Vatra will no doubt make every attempt to clear up these matters, but I earnestly ask of you that it not be allowed to be a permanent fact. I know nothing about the financial affairs of the Vatra other than that it is not a wealthy organization.

When I telephoned Bishop Noli and advised him of Faik Bey's assets and debts, Bishop Noli advised me that they would do their best. More than the fact that permanent payment of these debts by Vatra could cause a hardship, I should like to point out that King Zog's opponents in this country - and He has them - could make political capital out of the fact. Especially in view of Faik Bey's statement, in a letter of November 28, 1942, o Mr. Earl Brennan of the Office of Strategic Services (who had previously invited Bishop Noli and Faik Bey for an exchange of views on the Albanian situation), that His Majesty *"has become by the compelling force of events a symbol of Albanian independence - and has to be upheld at all costs if the past and the present are to be kept uninterrupted." In this same letter, in another passage, Faik Bey suggests that the United States "denounce the recognition of the Italian domination, implicitly granted in the appeasement days, and recognize King Zog as the lawful head of the country."*

More especially, I feel, the foregoing should be borne in mind in view of Faik Bey's recent acceptance to be King Zog's Personal Representative. It would do the cause no good whatsoever to invite more criticism from luke-warm friends and known enemies. Especially with such as Chekrezi loose. I believe he calls himself the moral representative of Albania, but, according to Faik Bey, he was neither moral (personally) nor representative of anything worthwhile.

As you will see in my letter to the Legation of Switzerland, Faik Bey left a valuable library. Many times Faik Bey has told me that he wished it to be part of the National Albanian Library. I earnestly hope this can be effected some day. Please pay my respects to Princess Myzejen, Princess Ruhie, and Princess Maxhide. Their Highnesses graciously invited me to have dinner with them when they were here in Washington. Please pardon my writing at such length, but since Faik Bey considered King Zog the Head of the Albanian Government, and you, Sir, His Minister, then I felt my report should be made to you. I am an American woman, but I shall always be interested in Albania ... and I hope Faik Bey's dream of a Free Albania will soon come true.

Accept, Sir, the assurance of my highest consideration,

Charlotte A. Graham,
Secretary to Faik Konitza

SSEES Naçi Collection 3/4

[57] Brussels1899

translated from French by Harry Hodgkinson

Memorandum On The Albanian National Movement[66]

by Faik Konitza, Brussels 1899

FIRST PART (Up to 1877)

I

Until 1877, very few Albanians had any idea that theirs should or could be a written language. It is true that in Northern Albania, and above all in Scutari, a number of merchants did make use of the Albanian language in corresponding with each other; and the Roman Office of Propaganda[67] had published a number of religious books in Albanian. But this initiative did not pass beyond its own narrow scope, and was not related to any national idea.

In Southern Albania, a similar initiative had been more successful. In 1827 the four Gospels had appeared in Albanian[68], in Greek script, and in a little time this book was in all Christian homes. The first edition had a print run of several thousands, and a second was issued in Athens in 1858.

II

Around the same time, an Albanian from Vithkuçi near Korçë, called Naum Veqilharxhi,[69] published an Albanian alphabet in Bucharest; and, back in Albania, sought to give a practical impetus to his initiative by setting up a school and propagating an inclination towards the national language; but, on being denounced to the religious authorities, he was, as all Albanians of the time thought, poisoned on the orders of the Patriarchate in Constantinople.

III

Another event proved happier for the Albanian language. About the middle of the century, J.Georg von Hahn,[70] Austrian Consul in Janina, wanting to learn Albanian, found two teachers: one called Apostoli, a surgeon by profession, and the other Kristoforidhi.[71] Then he set himself the task of travelling around the country to collect folksongs and stories. This interest shown by a foreigner in their national language impressed a number of Albanians, who resolved to cultivate it themselves.

IV

Further, one of Hahn's two teachers, Kristoforidhi, had already undertaken the collection of all Albanian words, in order to prepare a complete dictionary. Having been engaged by the London Bible Society in 1871, he published the next year an alphabet, a grammar, an abridged religious history, and so on.

However, the Greek Patriarchate was on the lookout for a suitable opportunity to uproot the Albanian language from the heart of the Albanian Orthodox, once and for all. One Sunday it organised a proclamation in all the churches that the Albanian language was the language of Protestants, Catholics, freemasons and atheists (since for the Orthodox these are interchangeable terms) and that in consequence one must take care not to handle the various Albanian books which were being spread around. From this time dates the stubborn and ineradicable hatred fostered for the national language by Orthodox Albanians – who are without doubt the most fanatical, stubborn, and least intelligent grouping in Albania.

From this angle, Kristoforidhi's books were a misfortune. But there was another side to it. Many Muslim Albanians were happy to buy these books, and I have seen them in many houses of Southern Albania. In any case, even if this opportunity had not presented itself, the Patriarchate would have looked for and found another.

V

An influence similar to Hahn's was exercised by A. Dozon,[72] the French Consul. Nothing surprised the Albanians who visited him, and set them thinking, so much as to see this foreigner writing their national language

VI

In brief, until 1877 a taste for the national language existed only in embryo and, above all, among people of a certain distinction. For despite the various revolts – notably against the Constitution of 1830 and those of 1854 and 1863 against obligatory military service, revolts concerned with a degree of autonomy – the question of the national language had not been raised in any serious fashion. One must move on to 1880 to find it so raised.

Second Part (1877 to 1884)

I

At this period an Albanian called Tahsin[73] lived in Janina. He was a very erudite man, who had lived for a long time in the company of scientists and men of letters in Paris: it was his affectation always to wear a turban. In 1877 he found himself in Janina and, having had an Albanian alphabet printed in Turkish script, he distributed it widely throughout Albania. He was allowed to go on doing this for some time, before being arrested and sent to Constantinople.

II

Tahsin's initiative was significant: it corresponded to a feeling of disquiet that Albanians as a whole began to experience. There was talk of the cession of Southern Albania to Greece; and as this rumour persisted, several intelligent Albanians realised that they had a language and national interests to defend.

A conference of Albanian notables was held in Constantinople, and there a decision was taken to send a number of delegates into Albania, to prepare people for an eventual uprising. One of these delegates, Abdul Bey[74], realised that a majority of Albanians of the south could be won over if one could persuade the *'babas'* or *'bektashi fathers'*, the dominant religion or sect, in the Tosk areas. It should be understood that these *'babas'*, formerly violently persecuted by the Turkish government, and even now enjoying only a very limited freedom, have always looked for a chance of liberating themselves. So Abdul Bey made visits to all their *'tekkes'* and (thanks to the co-operation of the Chief Baba, Alush de Frasheri, a kind of archbishop of this religion) had little difficulty persuading them to use their influence on the notables in favour of an eventual rising to achieve autonomy.

III

Meanwhile, events were hurrying forward. The Albanians kept the impetus going, and continued holding assemblies in Constantinople. The Sultan, suspicious at first, looked with favour on the Albanians until events took an unpleasant turn in Turkey. Thus Abdul Bey was sent once more into Albania, this time by the Sultan, to encourage (and also, some people said, to keep an eye on) the growing League, of which Prenk Bib Doda[75] and Hodo Bey were the moving spirits.

IV

I do not feel I need to talk about these events, because they are known and have been described in a good many books. But I will say a few words about one or two important facts which are not known:

i) The League of Southern Albania, led by Abdul Bey and Mehmet Ali Bey Vrioni[76] (as that of the North by Bib Doda and Hodo Bey) sent to all the southern beys the order to keep themselves and their people under arms, ready to set out at the lightest signal; and that if they refused, their houses would be burned, their goods confiscated, and themselves and all the members of their family executed; and if they did not preserve absolute security about this order the League, which had undercover members everywhere, would be fully informed of any treachery. This fact is certainly correct; for I remember that my father, who was alive then, had brought together from all around a great number of Albanians, and got ready to leave, on the day to be indicated, to carry out the order he had been given, which was to arrest the Turkish deputy governor, to occupy and fortify the square at Konica, to visit all the houses of pro-Greeks to secure any arms they might possess, and to proclaim the new government. After which, leaving enough men to give effect to the new authority, he was to go with his followers to a designated point, there to meet up with the other beys, who would have carried out a similar order in their own respective areas.

But private individuals, without official backing, cannot with impunity give orders to people of whom the majority either do not understand, or do not share, their opinions. So the methods of the League provoked extreme irritation among most Albanians.

ii) From day to day Abdul Bey became more authoritarian and more peremptory. He had gone to Libohova to demand 100,000 Turkish liras from Malik Pasha for the League[77], and when Malik Pasha promised him only 10,000, Abdul Bey threatened him, and said that when the revolution broke out, he would return to kill him and confiscate everything he had. Then the Albanians, who are far and away the most suspicious people on earth, began to ask themselves whether Abdul Bey did not have the ambition of making himself king. An amusing suspicion turned into a certainty for them: *'Yes, he did want to become king!'* Irritation simply grew. *'And who is it who wants to become king? A bey, and an 'unbreeched' bey at that, Abdul Dumé-Kérozi'* (that is to say, Abdul of the Scabby Dumé family). So the leading Albanians came to an agreement to countermand all Abdul Bey's projects, and from then on all the League's projects for action were a pitiable failure. It must be added that the suspicions against Abdul Bey seemed to be confirmed by what followed. There turned out in fact to be another claimant to the imaginary throne, Murad Bey Toptani. To prevent rivalry (so they say) Abdul Bey gave his niece in marriage to Murad. Hence alliance and peace were made between the rival houses.

V

Meanwhile, as these events were going forward in Albania, the Albanians of Constantinople, to give greater strength and staying power to their meetings, founded in 1879 a society which they called *'Drita' (Light)*.They immediately published the rules of the society in a widely-distributed brochure, and a reading book with an alphabet adopted by them.

All these publications were authorised by the Turkish government. The *'Drita'* Society, foreseeing the end of the League, determined to survive and carry on its work.

VI

Contemporaneous with the *'Drita'* Society at Constantinople, another society, *'The Voice of Albania'*,[78] was founded at Athens by Koulourioti.[79] Koulourioti occupies one of the most important places in the Albanian movement. Born in Greece, and orphaned at an early age, he was sent by the Greek Protestant Mission to America, where he distinguished himself in his college studies; then, turning to business, he made a large fortune in a few years. Back in Greece, he formed a committee, then an Albanian and Greek paper, *'The Voice of Albania'*, both of them frankly anti-Greek. He was accordingly persecuted everywhere: in restaurants and cafés, in shops where people refused to sell to him. He was blackguarded and stoned in the streets. In 1882, this Albanian patriot went to Albania to distribute nationalist books he had printed.

But the Greek consul had him arrested at Gjinokaster and he was sent back to Athens as a prisoner. All the same, he went on with his propaganda for several years; then he died after, it was said, having been poisoned. Koulourioti exercised an enormous influence. He inspired generous ideas, awoke the conscience of many, and produced the first example of an Albanian newspaper.

VII

Fortunately this example was copied. In 1884, the Constantinople *'Drita'* received from the Sultan Firman permission to publish an Albanian newspaper. This appeared, in fact, under the same name as that of the society, and appeared until 1885 (12 issues). Then the Turkish government, seeing that the paper was widely read, took umbrage and began to make difficulties. It was decided to transfer both the paper and the society's headquarters abroad. Bucharest was chosen, and one Uréto was sent there on behalf of the Albanians of Constantinople.

VIII

Something then happened to the society's advantage. A very rich Albanian merchant, Nicolas Naço,[80] had been living in Egypt for 30 years. Naço had a 15-year-old nephew whom he had left, during a short absence, at the Greek Consulate in Alexandria, where a friend of his, Krokhlihas, was Consul. Krokhlihas seemingly failed to comport himself morally, and Naço's nephew killed him with his revolver. Implicated in the case as an accomplice, Naço was sent to Greece with his nephew, having become naturalised as a Greek subject in Egypt. One must be aware of this detail to understand certain subsequent facts.

In Athens, Naço came to know Koulourioti, who persuaded him to work for a revival of Albanian national feeling. Acquitted by the court, Naço then left for Bucharest; going by way of Albania, where he did some propagandising.

IX

At Bucharest, Naço found the *'Drita'* Society, only recently established, already wholly in a state of disintegration. Parties had been created. One or two authors had sent manuscripts of books for publication; but the Albanians of Bucharest, notwithstanding the statutes of their society, would have nothing to do with them. They said: *'the manuscripts must be sent to Germany, where there are a number of Albanologists, to judge if they are worth printing.'* In brief, the general feeling was that they must make a pretence of keeping the *'committee'* in existence, otherwise the patriots would form one in earnest; that the Orthodox, even when Albanian speakers, would never wholeheartedly undertake any activity prejudicial to Greek interests and those of Russia; that the *'Turkish'* Albanians (that is, the Muslims) were insincere allies, who called for a pretence of national unity in order to reduce all the Orthodox again to a state of serfdom; and that, in sum, if it were necessary to call oneself Albanian, no opportunity should be lost to work behind the scenes in favour of religion rather than the national movement.

These things were said again and again at both public and private assemblies. And they corresponded so closely to the general feeling that it was decided to put up for public sale the type and the printing equipment the society had previously bought to publish at less expense all sorts of books.

X

A number of day-to-day happenings were to prove for certain the hostility of these Orthodox for their nationality. It was in this state of mind that a general assembly was convoked in 1885 at the instance of Naço, who had gained for himself a number of followers. It was in this assembly that one

Constantin Efthimi, a very rich Albanian and president of the society, spoke with great heat against the national movement and in favour of Russia, so that for sole response, Naço discharged a pistol shot at him.

Third Part (1885 to 1895)

I

Thus so far no serious attempt had been made to spread the idea of national identity in Albania. Initiatives of only short duration, and in consequence of little significance, had been made; and only one decisive fact had emerged – the creation of an overall society, which would bring together all the efforts, which would work uninterruptedly, publishing and publicising books and awakening the nation. But this effort had collapsed as soon as it had been born!

Naço, acquitted unanimously by a patriotic Romanian jury, hostile to Russian influence, set to work again. But he found very few supporters of his propaganda. This was because during his case, the pro-Slav party had reformed and consolidated itself, to achieve cohesion and start to grow. The head of this party was, and remains, an Albanian, Hercule Duro, both rich and very influential among the Albanians. Other parties were formed, notably a Greek party under the direction of another well-to-do Albanian Gavril Péma. But it must be noted, as we shall see further on, that these are mere subdivisions, and that all these parties are agreed on this essential point: that is, that Albania must come under an Orthodox power, never mind whether large or small, and that all propaganda must be directed to this end.

Accordingly meetings were arranged here and there. What exasperated the Greek-Slav party above all was that Naço showed himself as favouring Turkey; and that on the Sultan's birthday he went with two hundred Albanians to give a demonstration of loyalty in front of the Turkish Legation.

II

The *'Drita'* society, reconstituted by Naço, began to print and distribute

Albanian books. He also set up a Propaganda School where young people from Albania received a speedy and substantial briefing and returned to Albania.

One thing, though, harmed Naço and gave the Greek Slav party a field day: that intelligent and experienced as he was, and knowing six languages, he had learned all he knew by listening and observing, for he had not had even elementary instruction, and he only knew more or less correctly how to read and write. His opponents, although they knew little more than he did, brought this ignorance to light, and nothing discouraged the Albanians more than to tell them they were in touch with an ignoramus.

However, this did not prevent him from publishing an Albanian newspaper *'Shqipetari'* which appeared for more than a year, and was from beginning to end nothing but an attack on the Greeks and thc Slav states.

The Greek-Slav party, in a private meeting, decided to forward to the Russian Minister in Bucharest a declaration in which it was said, among other things, that the Albanians (that is, the Orthodox) would not work with Naço, who was an ignoramus and a vagabond; that they had the greatest respect for Russia, from whom they anticipated their salvation; and they begged the Minister to forward this expression of fidelity to his government, and to do with it and give it such publicity as seemed best to him. This declaration was signed by thirty or so Albanian notables.

III

About the same time, that is to say in 1887, Sami Bey Frashëri,brother of Abdul Bey and presently a member of the Council of State, obtained a firman permitting the creation of an Albanian school at Korça – a school whose upkeep was funded by *'Drita'.* At first the school roused great enthusiasm. Over 150 pupils attended, as many Christians as Muslims. But it soon wilted. On the one hand, a number of Albanians, at the instigation of the Turkish governor, began to make propaganda against the school, saying that the Muslims should not send their children to an infidel school; on the other hand the Greek bishop excommunicated all parents who sent their children to the school.

For the same reason, a number of other national schools which opened a little later, at Pogradec, Starove and Luaras, closed after operating for only a few months. However, the Korça school kept going, thanks to the energy of Orkhan Bey. At the present time, about 80 pupils attend; but all from poor and for the most part Christian families.

IV

The Albanians of Korça also set up a society. As the government wanted to forbid this, Alo Bey was chosen as president, and by this means the government yielded. And it is odd that for one or two years an Albanian society should have existed and held meetings in Turkey.

V

In 1892 a girls' school[81] was founded in Korça by a Protestant Mission. This school has had great success. All the notables, the Muslims above all, send their daughters there. At the last examinations (August 1898) the governor, the kadi and many others took part. For the young Muslim girls, there was a separate examination in which many ladies of the same religion took part. The Bible Society has the intention of setting up similar schools elsewhere. The purpose of this Mission is certainly not just religious; I think it is without doubt directed against the supporters of Slavism.

VI

To return to the Albanians of Bucharest. They went on with their quarrels and their propagandas, without being seriously organised, for sure, but putting all their efforts into it.In 1890 an Albanian from Korça, called Kocof, arrived in Bucharest from St Petersburg. His aim was to organise the Slav party among the Albanians. He proposed to the Albanians:

i) to arrange for the Russian government to give an annual subvention f or propaganda
ii) to write the Albanian language in Russian script
iii) words lacking in or lost from the Albanian language should all be taken from Russian, rather than be taken from Latin or created anew
iv) books should be printed on this basis.

In short, he proposed to turn the Albanian language into a demi-Slav dialect.

All this was received with enthusiasm, but it came to nothing. What one must never lose sight of, in discussing these Albanian parties, is that they had no organisation; that they were composed of ignorant merchants who had served in shops from the age of 15 to 25 or 30 before opening shops of their own and making their money; and that their idea of politics consisted in general of coming together and talking as though their wishes were reality. Further, it is very difficult to get the need for propaganda into such heads. They tell themselves that Russia and Greece have no need of propaganda, and that when the hour strikes, they will do what they want to do without hindrance. This state of mind is general among them.

Also, the representatives of the Russian government are very guarded with their maladroit partisans. And Kocof conceived such an impression of the Albanians of Bucharest that he did not follow up his project in any practical way. He was satisfied to distribute copies of an Albanian revolutionary march he had printed in Russia, and then left Bucharest.

VII

All the same, though these parties lacked true organisation they none the less kept in touch and propagandised. This is how they usually go about it: Every week Albanians – merchants, muleteers, and others – return to Albania. The committee of the Greek-Slav partisans go to see them: '*So, you are off! Good journey! In your native village are such-and-such notables: go to see them, and tell them to speak against the project for an Albanian school which is being proposed. Tell them that it is a new instrument of oppression which the 'Turkish' Albanians have created against us. Moreover, Orthodoxy is in danger. You, you go into another village. Bon voyage! Tell a notable so-and-so there that you have heard he had put out a recommendation in favour of Albanian schools. But isn't he in touch with what is going on? Doesn't he know that all the Orthodox have backed out of such projects, because they have recognised that they are a snare? You others, when you see somebody, tell him not to go on being friendly with Muslims pretending to be patriots, because he will end up in prison. All the 'Turkish' Albanians are the same: they profess to be patriots to get you to talk, then they pass everything on to the Governor, and you are arrested.*'

Hundreds of examples have acquainted me with this primitive and underhand propaganda of false patriots, whom the newspapers suppose to be so ardent on behalf of their nationality.

In 1888, Avramidhi Lakçe,[82] an Albanian, millionaire many times over, sent to the people of Korça an extract from his will, in which he left for Albanian schools many hundreds of thousands of francs – nearly half a million. The executors were some Christians and a Muslim, Orkhan Bey. Doctor Manci, one of the executors, to whom the copy of the will had been sent, called together his Christian colleagues and spoke thus to them: *'Avramidhi is leaving us 20,000 pounds if we would like to turn ourselves into Muslims. For he gives us Orkhan Bey as a colleague. Now I ask you: do you want to stay Christian and poor, or apostasise and make our town rich? – We don't want to become Muslims!'* they all replied, and they returned the will to Avramidhi, telling him that it could not be accepted. This uncouth interpretation of a will in no way concerned with religion is characteristic. It proves the state of mind of the Albanian Orthodox, and it is hard to expect anything from them. They are not to be persuaded, and it would require planned and powerful efforts to knock anything into their heads, not least a concept of nationality.

Fourth Part (1895 to 1899)

I

In 1895, I found myself in Paris, where I learned for the first time about the existence of Albanian propaganda in Bucharest and the printing of Albanian books there. However, I had been concerned in developing my (Albanian) language since 1890, and I had formed a small library of all the books printed by foreign Albanian experts. I had even begun to write a few articles on Albanian nationhood for a Paris newspaper. That is proof that of Albanian propaganda there was none. For I was one of the few who, on his own initiative, concerned myself with this question; and on many occasions I had spent holidays of two or three months in Albania, talking everywhere about the national question, received coldly by some, and with incomprehension by others – and despite my interest in this question I was unaware, and everyone I knew was unaware, of the existence of an Albanian movement.

The fact is (I have since observed, and there are a thousand incidents to prove it) that for the Albanians of Bucharest, and even for those of Constantinople, the national question did not exist: there was only a municipal question. For them, in fact, the aim of all patriotic efforts was the national future of the town of Korça – and nothing else.

II

I wrote to *'Drita'* to get hold of books, and when I had received them, I began to correspond with Naço. Thus we exchanged all our ideas about the future of the country. Some months afterwards, we decided to start an Albanian daily newspaper, and it was appropriate for me to go to Bucharest. But the money to cover the expenses we foresaw had not been accumulated – whether because the Romanian government thought the expenses too heavy for it to fund – for I believe Naço had made a request – or whether a major State highway Naço had undertaken and from which he hoped for big profits, had not lived up to his expectations – and we left the execution of our project for later.

However, while waiting I decided to begin on my own the publication of a periodical review which, to my way of thinking, should contain nothing but stories, poems and historical documents. In September 1896, therefore, I printed a prospectus-appeal which I circulated everywhere. It made a great impression, and I received hundreds of enthusiastic responses. However, I already had my reasons for thinking that the degenerate Albanian townsfolk were more enthusiastic in words than in deeds. I did not want to undertake this publication unless I could be ensured of making a go of it. And I expressed doubts about its success.

But I soon received a letter from Pandéli Évanghéli, president of *'Ditaria'*, who assured me that he would take it on himself to collect 400 subscriptions in Bucharest and 300 in the rest of Romania. The people of Constantinople promised 200 subscriptions, and those of Monastir (Bitolj) a contribution of 20 Turkish pounds a month. I have all these letters. To trust in them, I would soon be able to publish the review every week, and with illustrations. And why should one not have trust, since they were all serious people, for the most part public officials, and hence moved by an irresistible patriotism which risked compromising them in such an enterprise?

But we shall see that it was not a genuine enthusiasm. I may be forgiven if I stress somewhat the foundation of *'Albania'*, because I can show thereby the exact state of mind of the Albanians.

III

In 1895, I received a letter from a group of Albanians in Bucharest, saying they were glad to learn that I was concerning myself with the Albanian Question (I was once again in Paris); but that I ought not to compromise myself with Naço, *'a vagabond and an ignoramus'*; that I ought to be with them; and that they hoped to found a new society, *'Dituria'*. This society, when all is said and done, was no more than a venture by the Greek-Slav party. Pandéli Evanghéli, the most able and most active man of the party, was chosen as president. This is the same man who, a little later on, as I have already said, took the responsibility for the 700 subscriptions in Romania.

IV

As soon as the first number of the Review appeared, the heads of the Greek-Slav party got together for discussions. They were extremely annoyed at the anti-Greek slant of the paper. They then convened a meeting where they proclaimed: 1) that this review was an initiative on the part of tyranny and oppression, because the editor was a Muslim; 2) that people must be prevented from thinking that the propaganda was due to the initiative of *'Turkish'* Albanians; 3) that when the Greco-Turkish war broke out, such a paper could only prejudice Greek interests; 4) that there had moreover been attacks against Greek and Slav nationalities, and that nothing could justify such attacks.

Finally, some people thought the paper had received subventions from the Sultan to attack the Greeks. Others, that it was not an Albanian but a young

Turk paper, because there were attacks on the Sultan in it. These self-same jealous partisans of the Sultan reproached me several months later for talking of the Sultan in an unfriendly way.

It was decided at the end of the meeting:

1) not to take out subscriptions to *'Albania'*;
2) to set up an Albanian paper in Bucharest in opposition to mine, and also to show that the Orthodox were doing something. As a result, of the 700 subscriptions promised from Romania I received only 34, these from the more clever members of the party, who did not wish to draw attention to their hostility. An account of this meeting appeared in the Greek paper *'Patris'*, published in Bucharest.

V

The Albanians of Constantinople are, as we saw at the beginning of this account, zealous patriots. They have made a good deal of propaganda in Albania; but this has been confined to a rather restricted group: the Tosk-Albanian functionaries. Beyond that, their propaganda has been non-existent.

The Albanians of Constantinople are not concerned with politics, to which they are indifferent. For them, everything comes down to the question of the alphabet: in 1879 they adopted an alphabet created by Sami and Naim Beys (an alphabet of little practical use, as it cannot be printed because of certain special characters). Its authors put a relentless self-esteem to its presentation; for them everything is good which is printed in this alphabet, and everything bad which, being printed in another alphabet, seems to them to be challenging their glory as pioneers. So they greeted the appearance of *'Albania'* with great enthusiasm, as I said that it would subsequently be printed in their alphabet, so long the necessary funds were available to cut the type characters. Naim Bey, president of the Turkish censorship and of the Albanian Committee of Constantinople, even set himself down as one of my colleagues, and his are the verses published under the initials N.F. (Naim Frashëri)[83] and N.H.F.

But when they saw that the review went on being printed always in the same alphabet, for reasons I have made public, they changed their attitude, and while not going so far as to show hostility, they none the less had recourse to indifference.

In 1897, a clever student in Constantinople, Mehdi Bey,[84] did a lot of propaganda for the review, and became a trustee. In this capacity, he went to Ismail Bey Vlora[85] and other dignitaries of the Empire in Constantinople, and spoke to them on behalf of this nascent propaganda. He also distributed copies to people going by steamboat to Albania. But, nominated as attaché to the Governor of the Islands of the Archipelago, the Albanian Abeddin Pasha[103], he had to leave Constantinople. The son of Abdul Bey Frasheri, Midhat,[104] was another propagandist. One day (June 1897), on leaving the Austrian post office carrying a large packet of *'Albania'*, he was arrested by secret police agents. Held prisoner for three days at the Ministry of Police, he was set at liberty thanks to vigorous protests by his uncle Sami, a member of the Council of State. Some days afterwards, he was nominated attaché at the Sublime Porte. From then on, he was only timidly involved in Albanian propaganda.

I mention these two facts only to demonstrate one of the weakest points about this propaganda: it depended on luck. Strong today in one place, it would be weak or non-existent the next, because one or two patriots had left. Whereas on the Slav side people were exclusively occupied with propaganda.

Today (1899), Albanian propaganda in Constantinople is in the care of several students, of three or four Albanians from territories annexed to Montenegro in 1879, of several people from Scutari and from two or three officials in lower grades.

VI

Deceived by Bucharest, and let down by Constantinople, I turned to the people of Monastir.

They kept their word. They founded a kind of society, in order to raise funds and organise propaganda. The meetings took place in the house of Lieut.

Colonel Halid Bey, an Army doctor. Copies of the review were sent to the British Consul, who passed them on to those interested. I sent them openly by post, and they reached him. The Consul, who is now in Ankara, knew Albanian and read the paper with interest. Unfortunately, because of certain quarrels he was having with the Turks, he ceased to undertake receipt of the review. So for some time the review did not reach Monastir. Again, some zealous patriots left Monastir – above all a teacher at the *'Idahi'* school, Cherkét, who was nominated head of a similar school at Üsküt. However, soon afterwards the Bible Society of Monastir took upon itself to take several issues to pass on to their recipients.

VII

Such were the beginnings of this work. What were the subsequent developments, and what is the present state of Albanian propaganda? The paper started at Bucharest against *'Albania'*, under the name of *'Shqiperia'* was at first frankly hostile to me. But when the director was changed (following the circumstances outlined by me in *'Albania'* no. 9, A 159) the paper came into the hands of V. Dodani, an honest man and a patriot, who is not the tool of the Slav party, or the Greek and Italian, although equally he is not aware of the snares. In fact, he publishes the articles with which he is provided, and of which he does not understand the *'slant'*. He could do with a little more in the matter of intelligence.

VIII

However, he willingly lent his presence to a secret meeting at which about ten notables and the Serbian Consul at Bucharest took part. This took place in the month of May 1898. The Serbian Consul suggested an initial funding of 40,000 francs to start propaganda in favour of a rising in Albania to create an autonomous government linked with Serbia. But one of the people taking part, Gavril Péma, an intransigent pro-Greek, said that if there was only a question of money, it was more logical to ask for it from Greece; and next day he made public the secret of the meeting.

IX

Alongside the paper *'Shqiperia'*, another paper, *'Yll i Shqiperise' (Star of Albania)* had lately appeared in Bucharest. I rather encouraged the publication of this paper, and thought it would follow a good line. The man who principally took on the publication struck me as patriotic and intelligent. Unfortunately, others got mixed up in the paper, notably one George Meksi[86] (of whom I have spoken in *'Albania'*, A 159), and the paper suddenly made a violent Slavophile turn. According to a letter I recently received from Bucharest, the editors of this paper are in touch with the Russian Legation.

X

The attacks that *'Yll'* launched against *'Shqiperia'* led one to hope that these two papers might to a point neutralise each other. Further, *'Shqiperia'*, which was on quite good terms with us, came still closer as a result of these attacks: that, at least, was what I was led to think from a letter from the editor, V. Dodani.

XI

None the less, the propaganda of the Greek-Slav party against Austria did not die down so soon. And, on this subject, it is interesting to note how this propaganda is conducted.

The Albanians of Bucharest, aware of the weak point of their Orthodox compatriots, have adopted the tactic of spreading the rumour that the Austrian aim is to convert them all to Catholicism. This ridiculous allegation is their only weapon, but it is a strong one, and quite enough for such uneducated minds. On the other hand, they say to Albanian Muslims:

'As for us, we are Christians; it is therefore in our interest to go along with Austria, as a Christian power. But you, being Muslims, would pass into a state of slavery under this Christian power. That is why we lay aside our own special interest, regarding rather the general interest, and we say to you: take care, let us take care!'

Such is this perfidious and incessant, if irregular, propaganda. It must be said that it has little effect among Muslims, those in the movement being generally very sympathetic towards Austria. But its influence is very great among the Orthodox.

XII

In this regard, I made a number of strange observations during my last visit to Bucharest. We were given a splendid and enthusiastic reception, as if we were our country's saviours. This display would have been even greater, if I had not cooled it and caused some irritation by sending from the Vienna railway station a telegram announcing our arrival, not to the Greek-Slav committee, but to the Drita of Naço.

Arriving in Bucharest and seeing this enthusiasm, I said to myself: 'This is odd, and I find it surprising, coming from these ordinary and unconcerned tradesmen...' Nor was I wrong. Some days afterwards, it was suggested to me that I should carry on with *'Albania'* in Bucharest; that *'Shqiperia'* should cease publication, so that I could have all its readers; and that a management committee should ensure 10,000 francs a year for the papers.

In the many meetings we held, Murad Toptani explained an overall propaganda project. A number of specific reservations were made about insurgent bands. They were supported, but on condition that they attacked only Turkish officials, and not touching Bulgars and Greeks, as Murad proposed. With this reservation, the project was accepted, and it was resolved to continue with a funding of 150 to 250 thousand francs. But when Murad Bey raised the question of the headquarters of this propaganda effort, and told them that Dalmatia or Bosnia seemed most suitable to him, there was at once a glacial silence.

Finally, P. Evangheli said that they saw no objection to this, but there was a risk that funds would not be forthcoming under such conditions, *'because the other Bucharest Albanians are fanatics, and would not agree that the centre of the propaganda should be in a Catholic state'*. I took up a waiting attitude, as I realised that it was all quite useless, and the money would never be forthcoming. Nor was I mistaken. For four months they kept Murad Toptani there with promises that were never honoured. The only thing I obtained was the signature, in public session, of a telegram to the Sultan, whose text I had prepared.

XIII

With such a state of mind, an understanding could clearly be made easily between the Albanians of Bucharest and those who call themselves such in Italy. An understanding all the stronger in that the Italo-Albanians are Catholics, but of the Greek rite, and allow the marriage of priests (matters which bring them quite close to the Orthodox) – an understanding even stronger because they probably favour Montenegro in Albania, given the powerlessness of Italy. My view on this point is entirely shared by Murad Toptani.

The Italians do propaganda in southern Albania through the Albanians of Bucharest, and in northern Albania through the Italian Consulates. To their Albanian college and seminary at San Demetrio Corone and in Sicily – where, by the way, not a single word of Albanian is taught – they attract a certain number of young people, and so sustain in Albania a current of opinion in favour of the Albano-Italian colony. We may note in passing that: 1) appearances notwithstanding, there is complete agreement among Albano-Italians, as is proved by the fact that their alphabets are identical as to letters; 2) that they do not know how to speak Albanian. (Murad Bey confirmed this for me, as others had done.)

XIV

To widen the scope of their agreement, the Italians and the Albanians of Bucharest sought the support of those in Egypt. The Albanians of Egypt, who are quite numerous, are the richest merchants of Albania. They are in constant touch with their native land, and take an interest in the national movement. They have founded a society, *'Albanian Brotherhood'*, and recently proposed to publish an Albanian newspaper.

One of them, Efthim Mitko[87] published in 1878 *'The Albanian Bee'*, a collection of popular tales and stories: this is the best book so far published in the Albanian language.

But, set in a milieu far away from Orthodoxy, in daily contact with Westerners, their outlook is far from being as restricted as that of the other Albanian Orthodox. Moreover, despite the efforts of a certain Adhamidhi, a

Cairo doctor, representative of the Greco-Slav party in Egypt, no understanding has been reached between them and the Albanians of Bucharest. The situation of *'Albania'* in Egypt is, on the contrary, quite good.

XV

The Albanians of Bucharest have done better with those of Sofia. It is true that they, being mostly workers, cannot give much time to propaganda.

Moreover, there are two other parties in Sofia. Thus:
i) Albanian. This society is pro-Slav, and its seal is surmounted by a cross, thereby repudiating any purely national union, and making of the Albanian question merely a religious question. It has relations with 'Dituria' of Bucharest.

ii) The *'Bashkimi' (Unity)* society, run by Kristo P Stefan, who prints every year an almanac in the letters used in Constantinople. This almanac is edited by Midhat[88], son of Abdul Bey Frasheri – The *'Unity'* society is patriotic, and has the support of the Albanians of Constantinople. (Kristo P Stefan is at the same time one of our Sofia correspondents.)

ii) The Turkish paper Ittifak, edited by Yusuf Ali Bey. Yusuf Ali is from Kertchova, where Albanian and Bulgarian are spoken. So he speaks both languages, and has been able to win the confidence of both the Sultan and the Bulgars. Apart from a subsidy which it gives him, the Bulgarian government exerts, through the police, a pressure on Muslim Bulgars to subscribe to Ittifak, saying that it is their duty to educate themselves and abandon their gross ignorance. This extraordinary fact I learned both from letters from Bulgaria and by word of mouth from a friend of Y Ali living in Bucharest. It should be noted that, every time he goes to Bucharest, Y Ali is the guest of Duro. *'Ittifak'* is quite widely circulated in North East Albania.

XVI

The story of the various propaganda efforts has afforded the opportunity of speaking, on several occasions, of the state of mind of the Albanians. Now let us say a few words about the situation in Albania itself.

In general, Albanian officials in Albania are animated with the best feelings. Many can read and write Albanian. In the districts of Korça, Kolonia, Berat, nearly all the Beys keep up their language. In Elbasan, Monastir, and elsewhere there are a great number of them. It should be noted above all that young people in the schools are very interested in the national question. The country people, and above all the *'zaptiés'*, in the vilayet of Monastir notably, almost all can read.

In Northern Albania, the national movement is much less bright. I am talking above all of the Muslims. Nearly everyone there is even unaware that people have begun to write their language. However, among the Muslims of Dibra, Mat, Tirana, and the coastal towns, a national movement is beginning vaguely to take shape.

But, almost everywhere, Albanian schools would be well received. Among the towns where they are actively hoped for, one may mention Elbasan, Kolonia, Valona, Permet, Tepelen, Vertsche, Dibra, Ohrid, Tirana, Mati, and many small towns. Elsewhere, they would be received with an indifference which would quickly change into sympathy.

XVII

To conclude, there is in every Albanian head the germ of an idea, but this idea is neither old enough nor strong enough to get them into action. Why? Because at no time has there been a concern to develop these thoughts. The initiatives so far taken prove that educated Albanians have goodwill; but what are such initiatives by comparison with the tenacious, strong and well-organised efforts of the Slavs and the Greeks?

The number of those who read and understand, and have some influence, is small enough in Albania, and I can say that all of these have more or less read *'Albania'*; but beyond a certain point it is hard to find readers, because there are no more left who can read a newspaper fluently. By publishing articles in Turkish, one increases the number of readers, particularly in Northern Albania.The Albanian people are sufficiently awakened to show understanding, but one must bear in mind that nothing has been done to make them understand anything at all.

Caught between the Albanians of the North, who do not know how to read, and those of the South, who are suspicious, and see snares everywhere, the propagandist can only go forward through a thousand difficulties.

Collaborators, above all, are lacking. And the reason collaborators are lacking is the absence of schools. Where a school exists, there in effect is a nucleus for propaganda; and collaborators arise and take it on themselves to distribute publications. At Korça, quite some time ago, *'Albania'* was read in the cafés because from the moment an Albanian school existed, the Turkish government could not stop people reading Albanian.

One of the greatest difficulties in setting up schools is to find capable teachers. The Korça school was for a long time discredited, because for some time a tailor was put in as teacher, who knew just how to read and write.

What is needed is to set up a college, whether at Zara or Sarajevo, or in Albania itself (at Orosh, for example) with the double aim of quickly giving a substantial training to future teachers of Albanian, and of attracting young people of more or less influential families in order to give them – as is done by the Albanian college in Italy – a complete education.

That is a simple idea, after all. But what I wish to say above all is that day by day Austria engages greater sympathy among educated Albanians; and that if a means could be found of giving greater cohesion to these sympathies, a very strong movement would be created.

Fifth Part

An alphabetical list of all Albanians who, directly or indirectly, in favour or against, were involved in the patriotic movement, with a few words on each of them.

ABEDDIN PASHA: Former Minister of Foreign Affairs; at present Governor General of the Archipelago. A good patriot, but cautious.

ALO BEY (KORÇA): Dealt in leeks as a young man; later turned himself into an intermediary between Turkish officials and anyone who had a case to settle. He is actually a protector of brigands, whom he furnishes with victuals and shelter in winter. They share the profits, and in this way he has become rich and quite powerful. He is a patriot in the sense that he does not want to see the government infringe local liberties; has often been linked with the pro-Slav faction, and the Russian consul in Monastir stayed with him on his last trip to Korça: but all that is to give him importance in the eyes of the Turkish government.

AHMET BABA OF K: Bektashi monk and excellent patriot. He was deported to Tripolitania, whence he escaped with Murad. (A curious detail: he dresses like us, and wears a hat since going to Italy – and now in Corfu: which shows how the Bektashis, even when monks, differ from Muslims.)

AKIF BEY: nephew of Dervish Bey, a moderate patriot.

DERVISH BEY: An ardent patriot, but not very bright, and awkward. (His sister married a Urioni, and she is a great propagandist for Albanian, which she writes and cultivates, among the women of Berat.)

DUÇI Nicolas: originally from Korça, a prominent merchant, the most important and most patriotic of the Albanians of Egypt. He is president of the *'Albanian Brotherhood'*. (His son, Michael Duçi, has written verses for *'Albania'*, which he encourages in Egypt.)

DODANI Visarion (Bucharest): honest man, patriotic, rich, vain, of moderate intelligence; he took the newspaper *'Shqiperia'* in hand, half for patriotic reasons, and half so that he could become involved with the journalist-deputies of Romania.

DEMIR BEY PEKINI: Unconcerned with everything. The Tanzimat (Constitution), which suppressed seignorial privileges, seems not to have affected him. He levies taxes when he is in need of money. (Married an aunt of Murad Bey.)

DAUT: Bektashi Sheh of Tepelen: Has patriotic sentiments.

DATZ Shapir aga: patriot of Dibra; fought vigorously against Demir Pasha when he was sent by the Sultan to disarm the country.

DURO Hercule: a threefold millionaire; none the less he still runs four or five grocery shops. He was born in the village of Boboshtica (Korça) and lives in Bucharest. (His father, Zhemeli Duro, who died two years ago, was an ardent patriot.)

EVANGHELI Pandeli: originally from Kolonja; very intelligent, pliant and able. His voice preponderates among the Albanians of Bucharest. Is strongly pro-Greek, but would favour Russia quite as much, since his whole aim is Orthodoxy.

VISARION: Orthodox Bishop of Elbasan: Was an ardent Albanian until the Russian agents arrived at Shpat and Elbasan (February/March 1897).

GHECIO: one of the Bucharest millionaires. All the same, his avarice prompts him to oppose any enterprise of a national character, so that he won't have to make a contribution towards it. Otherwise, he is an intolerant Orthodox.

GOSTIVARI Bey: compared with other chiefs from his part of the country, he is a patriot. His son Kiamil is one even more. They have great influence in the area. Kiamil recently married the daughter of an Üsküt chief. (Kiamil assumes, voluntarily, the role of head of the Gostivar telegraph bureau; when, which happens rarely, a telegram is to be sent off, he operates the machine in the presence of several friends, and he passes for an expert.)

HAMDI Bey: the best of the Albanian patriots. So much so that if he should come out of prison, after so many years of preventive detention, he will certainly start propagandising again. Grandson of Ilias Pasha. His family have great influence in Dibra. He was arrested as a result of a denunciation by the Orthodox *'patriots'* of Bucharest.

HALID Bey: Lieutenant-Colonel, Army doctor at Monastir. Excellent patriot, who spread his ideas among the people around him.

HUSREF Bey (at Starove): Same origin and same type as Alo Bey, but less dishonest. Supports the Albanian school which has been operating for two years in Starore.

HARITON Thanas: One of the Bucharest notables. Honest, stubborn, and a little simple. Goes into raptures about *'true and well-lit paths'* and is always repeating that Albania must *'get there'*, never mind how. (Originally from Korça.)

IBRAHIM Edhem: Originally from Kolonja; secretary of the Bank of Salonika in Constantinople, where he is tireless in making propaganda.

ILO Dhimitri: lawyer, edits the paper *'Yll i Shkjiperise'*. Has neither patriotism nor any conviction at all. He is despised by everybody, not only because of his infirmity (for his nose was completely chopped off by a stone which once fell on his face) but also for his untrustworthiness. He received for his paper, monthly: 1) A hundred francs from the management of the Greek paper *'Patris'* of Bucharest; 2) a subvention (probably) from the Russian government; 3) a sum (certain) from Albanians involved in business in Odessa.

IONUS Aga: Patriot of Üsküt. Has influence. Cannot read.

ISMAÏL PASHA, of Elbasan. One of the three or four richest Muslim Albanians. Is rather on the side of the government, though he does not oppose the national movement.

ISSOUF ALI BEY: Editor of the *'Itifak'* at Sofia; cares for nothing but money. At present money comes to him from the Sultan and from Bulgaria.

KERITZA Mihail: Albanian-Vlach, one of the Albanian notables of Bucharest; an unremitting supporter of Greece.

KOLÉA Sotir: of the Commercial Company of Salonika Ltd. A good patriot, and well-informed. For five years he has been preparing a great Albanian dictionary. Sometimes writes for *'Albania'*.

KYRIAZI: Albanian from Korça, Bible missionary at Monastir. Ardent patriot. Recently published a bulky Albanian manual of arithmetic under the pseudonym Athanas Sino.

KARDHO Mandi: Nephew of Duro; merchant, like all the Albanians of Bucharest. Ardent patriot.

KUNÉSHKA Vani: Friend and colleague of Kardo. Patriot. (These two Albanians are among the strongest supporters of Austria at Bucharest.)

KARBUNARA Dudé (Berat): Friend of Islam Bey Vrioni. Wanted to set up an Albanian school some years ago. Passes for a patriot.

KOSTURI (I forget his forename; I think he is Vasil Kosturi.) Merchant of Korça, where he lives. He is the leader of those Korça people who sincerely want Albanian unity without distinction of religion. An honest man, somewhat reserved.

LUARASI Dzafer: Lives at Korça, relation of Naim Bey. A true patriot, but somewhat timid.

MOLÉ Dhimitri: Originally from Korça. Merchant at Philippopolis. One of the rare Orthodox who is neither pro-Greek nor pro-Slav. Makes good propaganda, when he spends a month or two in Albania.

MIDHAT: Son of Abdul Bey. Secretary or attaché at the Sublime Porte. Active and intelligent young patriot. Has written several articles for *'Albania'*. Has translated the life of William Tell into Albanian. Favours Austrian influence very much.

MEHDI BEY FRASHERI: Attaché to the Governor-General of the Archipelago; very keen young patriot; showed remarkable activity when he was in Constantinople, where propaganda is to be made among 50,000 Albanians.

MAHMUD PASHA of Elbasan: Patriot, but cautious. One of his three daughters married General Saadeddin Pasha (a Turk). His son-in-law is son of the (word illegible) Ali-Sait Pasha; and when this Minister of War was alive, Mahmud had considerable power.

MEHMED-ALI Pasha of Delvino: Governor of Korça; belongs to the oldest family of Delvino; great grandson of Selim Pasha of Delvino. A decent man, with affable manners, and patriot in a relative fashion. He said, on arriving in Korça: *'I don't want any religious divisions and quarrels. You are all Albanians.'*

NAIM BEY: Brother of Abdul Bey. President of the Censorship Commission; ardent patriot, author of most of the books published in Bucharest. Has been ill for five years. Always speaks of Austria in the warmest terms.

NAUM KRISTAKI: Albanian from Korça, landowner in Romania. Would be well inclined to spend several thousand francs a year on propaganda, if the Greco-Slav party did not worry him with endless intrigues.

NAÇO Nicolas: Ardent patriot, speaker, and able propagandist. His defect is being a bit of a bragger, and vain. Contractor for State roads. Receives a subvention for his school from the Romanian government. Is a supporter of Austria.

NASUH Effendi, at Kolonja: former examining magistrate at Monastir. Keen and influential patriot. Comparatively rich for the neighbourhood.

ORKHAN Bey, son of Cecis Bey: One of the best of the Korça patriots. Has been a keen supporter of the Albanian school.
PEMA, Gavril: Head of the pro-Greek party in Bucharest. Has a certain disdain for his political friends, since they are merchants and he is a manufacturer. Comes from Korça.
REDZEP Pasha, Marshal: Seven years ago he asked for an audience with the Sultan, and asked him to do something for Albania. The Sultan promised him a reply next day, and two days later Redzep Pasha was exiled to Baghdad, under cover of his appointment as Commander of the 6th Army Corps.
RIZA Bey, son of Halil Pasha of Monastir. Counsellor of State. A patriot, but not so far as to risk his position.
SAMI Bey: Counsellor of State; brother of Naim, but less of a patriot than him. Has published an Albanian grammar.
SHEFKET Bey: Head of the Turkish College of Üsküb. Ardent and genuine patriot, but timid. Has published an article in *'Albania'* (A 41).
SPIRO Dina: Merchant at Shibin-El-Korn (Egypt). Passes for a patriot, although he took for himself, along with Vréto, 800 Turkish pounds (17,000 francs), which the will of an Egyptian Albanian had bequeathed for Albanian schools.
SHAHIN Bey: Native of Kolonja. (Recently nominated as deputy governor of a district in the vilayet of Monastir. I haven't received any news of him since he left Constantinople.)
SHIROKKA Filipp: Engineer-draughtsman, native of Scutari. Presently in Cairo. Ardent and well-informed patriot. He is our best Albanian writer. Assiduous collaborator with *'Albania'*, under the pseudonym of Geg Postripipa.
SARAC Ismail Bey: One of the best-known patriots of Dibra.
SALIH Bey: At Durazzo; (I think he is from Schiak). He formerly asked Dr. Thémo that we should print an alphabet. He proposed to arrange for the opening of a school.
SELIM Bey, of Delvino: First cousin of Mehmed Ali Pasha (see above). Has no patriotism, but knows the way the wind blows. Very influential, and also one of the most intelligent and nice Albanians. He is called '*the diplomatist of the Laberie*'.
SPIRO KIOSÉ SOLHAK: The delegate from Shpat to Constantinople, in

1896, to present a petition to the Embassies of Austria and Russia. (This petition was drafted by Murad Bey.) Spiró Kiosé is a patriot and moreover an able man. He is the person most capable of doing propaganda in Central and Southern Albania.

TOPTANI, Murad Bey: Ardent patriot, quite intelligent, but without following things through (sans esprit de suite). He is, with the Marquis of Aletta, one of our two candidates to an imaginary throne. Son-in-law of Naim Bey. Abhors the Slavs, and is very sympathetic to Austrian influence.

TOPTANI, Réfik Bey: His brother; as good a patriot as Murad, he is better informed.

THOMA, Abrami: Ardent patriot, and a passable writer. Taught for some time at the Albanian school in Korça.

TARPO Brothers: Three brothers in Bucharest, under of Dodani. Less given to intrigues than anyone else. Their house at Korça is used to house the Albanian school. One of the three, Petri, who has no children, will leave (so it is said) several hundreds of thousands of francs to Albanian schools. Gergio Christian, son of the eldest of the foregoing, is a student in Berlin, and a good patriot from whom much is to be hoped.

Dr. THÉMO: Excellent patriot, formerly Army major, left Constantinople in secret because he was suspected of being a Young Turk. Actively involved in Albanian propaganda. At present a doctor (municipal doctor) in the town of Médschidié.

TZIKO: Suli family, emigrated to Padua about the beginning of the century. Have nothing to do with the Calabrians and Neapolitans. But all the same, good patriots.

VLORA Fénd Bey: Known for his vengeances by means of false denunciations. On several occasions he set himself against the national movement. Presently Vali of Konya.

VLORA Suréia Bey: Kinsman of the above; had intelligence contacts with Italy and was arrested and sent to Constantinople – the exact date I don't know.

VLORA Ismail Bey: Kinsman of the previous couple; member of the Council of State, a man of great worth and of dignity, and not lacking in patriotism. Married a Bulgarian (wrongly thought to be a Greek).

VLORA Dzémil Bey: Son of Selim Pasha and kinsman of the preceding three. One of the young patriots with most zeal and intelligence. (He proposes to come to Brussels for a few days.)

VRIONI: In general, all members of this family are patriots; but above all Islam Bey, Salih Bey – who is preparing a small dictionary – and his son Nuzhet. (The late Mehmed Ali Vrioni Pasha was a much-appreciated satirical poet. He used to improvise very cutting epigrams in Albanian. He was very active with Abdul Bey in 1880.)

VRÓTO: Originally sent by the Albanians of Constantinople to found *'Drita'* in Bucharest. Has written two or three pretty bad books. Receives a small pension from the Greek-Slav party to make propaganda against the Albanian language, and to say that only the Greek and Slav languages are worth anything. Aged between 80 and 84.

ZOGOLLI Dzemal Pasha: Vice-governor of Mati, where he has powder mills. Good patriot, but does not understand the need for schools.

ZOGOLLI, Dzelal Bey: Brother of the foregoing. Equally patriotic. These Albanians have great influence.

CAS. HH Archive

Memoire sur la Mouvement National Albanais
Bruxelles Janvier 1899
House-Hof und Staatsarchiv -Wien
Karton 18 der Grupe XIV (Albanien) Folio 358r-401r

Obtained from the Vienna Archive by Dr. Ihsan Toptani

[58] December 1942

Funeral Oration Of Faik Konitza

Delivered by Bishop Fan Stylian Noli
Boston, Mass., Dec. 20, 1942

Ladies and Gentlemen:

We are gathered together here to pay our last respects and say farewell to one of the ost distinguished sons of Albania, Faik Konitza. As you all know, Faik Konitza was one of the greatest champions of Albanian independence. He was certainly the greatest master of Albanian prose-writing. Moreover, he is the man who re-discovered the old Albanian flag of Skanderbeg. These are three titles which even his bitterest opponents would not dream of denying him.

Albanian Flag

Let me add a few words about the Albanian flag. As you all know, none of the flags of our Balkan neighbours are older than a century and a half. Some of them are less than a century old. Ours is at least 500 years old and perhaps several centuries older. It was the flag of George Castriot Skanderbeg, the national hero of Albania, who fought against the Turks for a quarter of a century and was the last Christian warrior in the Balkans to defy successfully the greatest Sultans of Turkey. After Skanderbeg's death Albania, abandoned by the European powers, had to groan for four centuries and a half under the yoke of the unspeakable Turk. During that period Skanderbeg's flag was forgotten – nobody knew of its existence until a young scholar dug it up in a library from a Latin biography of Skanderbeg by Barletius. That scholar was Faik Konitza and that flag over his coffin, the red flag with the black double-headed eagle, is the one he re-discovered.

Education

From what I have said, you can imagine that he was a highly educated man. He was trained in French schools and received his Bachelor's Degree at the College de Lisieux, University of France. Later on, he received is Master's Degree at Harvard University in the Romance Languages. He was not satisfied with degrees, but throughout his whole lifetime he collected and read books, and never forgot anything he read. As a matter of fact, he was a walking encyclopaedia.

Career

At the age of 26 he began to publish his review *'Albania'* in Brussels, in French and Albanian. He continued that publication until 1909, when he came to America. His review is a treasure house of Albanian history, literature, philology and folklore. It is written in beautiful style and is the most enduring piece of work he has left us. Harvard University has a complete collection in Widener Library where it can be consulted. In America, he served as editor of the Albanian newspaper *'Dielli'* and as President of the Albanian Federation *'Vatra'*.

In connection with his journalistic work, you all know that he was not exactly an angel, as he sometimes dipped his pen in vitriolic acid in true French fashion. But, after all, no one is perfect, and we will just let bygones be bygones. In 1926, he was appointed Minister Plenipotentiary of Albania by King Zog, and remained at that post until 1939, the fatal year when Albania was invaded by Italy on Good Friday.

Last Act

After the Italian occupation of Albania, Mr Konitza was notified by the State Department that he could not enjoy diplomatic privileges any longer because Albania had ceased to exist. The Albanian Legation in Washington was closed. It was the period of appeasement policy, but since 1939 things have changed. War broke out, Mussolini was not appeased but joined Germany, and finally the United States was forced into war by Pearl Harbour. Moreover, the Albanians were doing some real fighting and could be helpful to the United Nations. And so, as a recognition of their bravery, came that fine statement of the Secretary of State Mr Cordell Hull on the 10th of this month by which Albania was assured of regaining her independence under the Atlantic Charter.

King Zog took Mr Hull at his word, reappointed Mr Konitza as his representative in Washington, and applied for official recognition as the head of the Albanian government-in-exile. Mr Konitza wrote immediately to the State Department in the name of King Zog regarding this recognition and that was Koniza's last act. He died a few days later, ands so he never received the answer from the State Department. But there are so many of us waiting, and we hope that before long the answer will come, and we are quite sure that the answer will be favourable. Mr Hull, in his historic statement of Dec. 10 concerning Albania, said: *"Consistent with its well-established policy not to recognise territorial conquest by force, the government of the United States has never recognised the annexation of Albania by the Italian crown."* If that pronouncement has any meeting at all, it means that the United States still recognises King Zog and not the King of Italy as the head of the Albanian government.

Fine Gesture

There is more evidence that the answer of the State Department will be favourable. The American government has decided to send Mr. Konitza's remains to Albania in due time at the end of the war. Such courtesies are usually extended only to foreign diplomats who die in active service. This means that Mr Konitza is recognised as the representative of the Albanian government who died in active service. However it may be, we deeply appreciate that noble gesture of the American government, and we know that Faik Konitza deserves it. He deserves to find eternal rest in the country he served all his life so faithfully and so loyally. May God Almighty grant him eternal peace.

CAS. D.D. archive
Originally published in *'Dielli',*
December 20 1942

Notes

1. William E. Gladstone (1809-1898)
English statesmen and author, very anti-Ottoman and the greatest supporter of the Greeks, Bulgarians, Montenegrins and Serbs

2. Theodor A. Ippen (1861-1935)
Austrian diplomat, based in Shköder, was adviser to Austro-Hungarian Ambassador to London during the Ambassador's Conference in London in 1912-1913. Theodor Ippen published two books about Albania and was in correspondance with Konitza. See biography in German by Anneliese Wernicke *'Theodor Anton Ippen'*, 1967, Wiesbaden

3. Baron Agenor Goluchowski (1849-1921)
Born in Galicia of Polish origin. His father Count Agenor Goluchowski, the elder(1812-1875) was the Austrian Minister of the Interior, 1859-1860. Minister at Bucharest 1887-1893, Minister for Foreign Affairs of Austro-Hungary from 1895 to 1906.
See more in: F.R. Bridge, 'The Habsburg Monarchy among the Great Powers, 1815-1918'

4. Shahin Bey Kolonja (1865-1919)
One of the leading Albanian figures in Bulgaria and Turkey. He was the editor and publisher of *'Drita'*, a periodical published in Albanian with occasional articles in Greek,Turkish and French. *'Drita'* was sponsored by Habsburg Monarchy.

5. Visarion Dodani (1857-1939)
Born in Albania. In 1880, he emigrated to Bucharest when he became a member of the *'Drita'* society. He edited and published the periodical *'Shqiperia'* between 1897-1899. He was in correspondence with Konitza, Pashko Wasa, Naim Frasheri and Thimi Mitko etc. The famous Albanian poet, Lasgush Poradeci (1899-1897), was very crtitical of his *'patriotism'*.
See more in: 'Lasugh Poradeci', Publicistika Onufri, Tirana 1999, pp.144-320

6. Murat Bey Toptani (1868-1917)
Poet, sculptor and friend of Konitza, he married a daughter of Naim Frasheri (1846-1900).

7. Hasan Zyko Kamberi
The XVIII century Albanian poet. Born in Starje-Kolonja in Albania. His most famous poem is *'Paraja'*. The only manuscript of his collection was lost.

8. Drita (1901-1908)
The Albanian periodical published by Shahin Bey Kolonja

9. Gasper Jakova Merturi (1870-1941)
Albanian nationalist from Shkodër, of Kosovan origin, very much anti-Konitza. In an 1905 edition of *'Albania'*, Konittza published some very hostile letters about him.

10 Kristo Floqi (1873-1950)
Most celebrated Albanian dramatist. He studied law in Athens and then emigrated to USA where he became editor of *'Dielli'* and was co-founder of *'Vatra'* with Faik Konitza and Fan Noli. He was arrested by the communists and died in prison.

11. Lef Nosi (1876-1945)
One of the greatest Albanian nationalists, he was amember of the first Albanian Cabinet in 1912. He was killed by the new regime in Tirana in 1945.

12. Nikolla Bey Ivanaj (1879-1951)
An Albanian nationalist from the Gruda tribe. Published the weekly newspaper *'Shpnesa e Shcypenis' (The Hope of Albania)* from 1905-1908, in Albanian, Italian and Croatian.

13. Dervish Bey Elbasani
Born in Elbasan. An Albanian nationalist and a very good friend of Konitza . He died in Syria after the Second World War.

14. Mary Edith Durham (1863-1944)
Artist, antropologist, journalist, traveller and champion of Albanian independence. Born in London in 1863. Studied at Bedford College and the Royal Academy. In 1900, she went to Montenegro for the first time. Henceforth, she was very much connected to the Balkans. She wrote 2000 letters on behalf of the Albanians. Her books include: *'Through the Lands of the Serb' (1904), 'The Burden of the Balkans' (1905), 'High Albania' (1909), 'The Struggle for Scutari' (1915) 'The Twenty Years of Balkan Tangle' (1921), ' The Sarajevo Crime' (1925), 'Some Tribal Origins, Laws,& Customs of the Balkan' (1928)*. She was the Balkans correspondent for The Times, The Manchester Guardian and The Near East from 1911-1914.

15. Saint Jerome.
Of Ilyrian origin, he translated the Bible into Latin for the first time.

16. Pope Clement XI
Of Albanian origin

17. Scanderbeg Gjergj Kastrioti (1403-1468)
Albanian national hero.
See 'Scanderbeg' by Harry Hodgkinson, Centre for Albanian Studies, London 1999

18. Fan S. Noli (1882-1965)
Albanian poet, writer, priest and Albanian prime minister. Born in Turkey 1893. In 1908, in Boston, Noli established the Albanian Autonomous Orthodox Church.
See Robert Elsie 'History of Albanian Literature', 995 Vol I. pp. 373-383.

19. George J. Goschen (1831- 1907)
From 1901, Lord Goschen of Hankhurst. British Diplomat and statesman of German origin. In 1880, he became H.M. Ambassador to Turkey. He recommended a united Albania in his reports to the Foreign Office.

20. Petty-Fitzmaurice, Edmund George, Baron Fitzmaurice, of Leigh (1846-1935)
Statesman, diplomat and historian, he was born in Lansdowne House. Educated at Eton, where he won a Prize for French and at Trinity College, Cambridge, where he was a scholar. M.P. and Under-Secretary for Foreign Affairs. In 1880, he was appointed commissioner for East Roumelian Commission under the Treaty of Berlin. He recommended the formation of a greater Albania.

21. Aubrey Herbert (1880-1923)
British diplomat, M.P., traveller and journalist. Second son of Lord Carnarvon. In 1912 -1913, he was president of The Albanian Committee; in 1918, he became the president of the Anglo-Albanian Society. The greatest champion of Albanian independence.

22. Trieste Congress
Organised by The Habsburg Monarchy in 1913. Faik Konitza was elected the president.

23. Marquis de San Guiliano (1853-1914)
Italian Minister of Foreign Affairs

24. Burney, Sir Cecil, British Admiral (1858-1929)
In 1913, he was the Commander of International Forces in Shkodër, Albania

25. Essat Pashe Toptani (1863-1920)
A controversial figure in Albanian history. He was born in Tirana and was in charge of Turkish gendarmerie in Shkodër up to 1908, when he became a member of the Union and Progress Party. Brother of Gani Bey Toptani from the well-known Toptani family of Tirana.

26. J.D. Bourchier (1850-1920)
The legendary Balkans corespondent of The Times

27. Levenon Gower.
A Times journalist who spent some times in the Balkans

28. Mehmet Bey Konitza
Elder brother of Faik Konitza. Ex-Turkish diplomat. In 1920, became Albanian Ambassador to London. Adviser to King Zog on Balkan issues, he died in Rome after World War II.

29. Wilhelm, Furst von Albanian, Prinz zu Wied (1876-1945)
See:Denkschrift uber Albanian von Wilhelm, Furst von Albanian Prinz zu Wied.

30. Father Gjergj Fishta (1871-1940)
One of the greatest Albanian poets and writers. Born in Zadrima in northern Albania. He was educated in Albania and Bosnia . He wrote many books. In 1919, he was elected a member of the Albanian delegation to the Paris Peace Conference.He was elected as MP for Shkodër in the new Albanian parlament. He was elected a member of the Itlalian Academy of Arts and Sciences in 1939.

31. S. Curani (1856-1941)
Albanian patriot of Shkodër iin Albania.

32. Angjelin Suma
From a well-known family in Shkodër in northern Albania Was for many years the British Vice-Consul in Scutari (Shkodër)

33. Çoka
From an influential Catholic family from Shkodër

34. Hans Delbruck (1848-1929)
German historian

35. Theodor Mommsen (1817- 1903)
Historian of Rome. He edited the monumental *'Corpus Inscriptionum Latinarum'*. His greatest work remains his *'History of Rome'*. He was awarded the Nobel Prize in 1902.

36. Wilhelm von Jagow Gustav (1813-1871)
German statesman

37. Field-Marshal August von Mackensen (1849-1945).
German military figure

38. J.V. Goethe (1749-1832)
German poet and author of *'Faust'*

39. Count Nikolaus Pavlovich Ignatiev (1832-1908)
Russian diplomat and statesman

40. Otto Ed, L. von Schon Bismark (1815-1898)
German Chancellor. At the Congress of Berlin, he claimed that the Albanians were not a nationality. Such a statement was not all suprising as Prince Bismarck was also apparently unaware of the existence of both the Dutch and the Danish nations.
See ZHC2/218

41. Parashqevi Qiriazi (Kyrias) (1880-1970)
Her great contribution was on education in Albania. She the sister of Sevasti Qiriaz.

42. Kristo Dako (1878-1941)
Great Albanian patriot. Journalist, historian of King Zog and propagandist of Albanian affairs. He married Sevasti Qiriazi.

43. Dervish Hima (1873-1928)
Albanian nationalist and very anti-Turkish. Member of the *'Black Hand'*, founded in 1878.

44. Armin Sasvari (1853-1924)
Born in Tormas in Hungary, he was the editor of *'Revue d'Orient et de Hongrie Foszerkesztoje'*, 1886-1898.

45. Mary Herbert (1889-1970)
Widow of late Aubrey Herbert. A great friend of Albanians. She refounded the Anglo-Albanian Assotiation in 1943, with help from Edith Durham, Dervish Duma and Anton Logoreci.

46. Vatra
Organisation founded in 1912 by Fan Noli, Faik Konitza, Kristo Floqi and others which played a critical role in the creation of the Albanian state.

47. William Martin Leake (1777-1860)
English classical scholar, topographer, diplomat and army officer. His great work is *'Researches in Greece'* (London 1814).

48. Dervish Duma (1908-1998)
Former Albanian diplomat, Chairman of Anglo-Albanian Association, 1994-1998. Born in Borsh in Albania, educated in Albania and London at the L.S.E. Was in correspondence with Faik Konitza, Edith Durham, General Percy, Robert Hodgson etc.

49. Ahmed Bey Zogolli (1895-1961)
President and then King of the Albanians from 1928-1961, who died in Paris in 1961.

50. Constantin Chekrezi(1892-1959)
Born in Albania, studied at Harward University. Published the first Albanian-English dictionary, *'Albania Past and Present'* etc. Established newspaper in Albania and USA. President of Free Albanian Committee. Very hostile to King Zog.

51. Sumner Welles
USA State Departament Secretary during 1942-1944.

52. Tajar Zavalani (1903-1966)
Journalist, historian and translator. Educated in Albania, Greece, Italy and USSR. Sometime press secretary to King Zog, a very good friend of Chekrezi in USA.

53. Anton Logoreci (1910-1990)
Prominent journalist and BBC commentator, from a very important family in Shkodër. A passionate Albanian nationalist.

54. **Perlat Bogdo,**
Born in Albania, educated in Albania and London. A close friend of Chatin Sarachi.

55. Chatin P. Sarachi (1903-1974)
Albanian diplomat and painter. Was very good friend of King Zog up to 1940. Very good friend of Paul Getty and Oscar Kokoscha. From 1941, became very hostile to King Zog.

56. General Joselyn Percy (1880-1958)
In charge of the Albanian gendarmerie during the King Zog regime

57. Lord Noel Buxton (1862-1948)
Labour M.P. From 1945, President of the Balkan Committee. A good friend of the Bulgarians. *See 'Noel Buxton- a Life' by Mosa Anderson, London, 1952*

58. Sir Robert Hodgson
Former British Ambassador to Albania

59. Kerran F L
A German, naturalised British subject,Labour M.P., closely connected to King Zog, whom he saw several times a week.

60. Qazim Kastrati (1905-1974)
Onetime private secretary to King Zog, who later became the Secretary of National Liberal Club.

61. Sir Edward Boyle (1878-1945
Former president of the Balkan Committee

62. Sotir Martini
Minister of Royal Court of Albania who was very close to King Zog

63. Rev Peter Kolonja
From 1942, he was intermittently King Zog's representative in the USA.

64. Hulusi Kavo
One of the editors of *'Dielli'*

65. Vandeleur Robinson
While working for the Political Inteligence Department, he was very much involved with Albania.

66. Notes by Harry Hodgkinson
This manuscript is a valuble source of knowledge of the personalities and Albanian nationals involved in the rise of the Albanian nationalism between the Treaty of Berlin and the Balkan Wars.

67. Congregatia de Propaganda Fidde
See R. Elsie 'History of Albanian Literature', vol. I, pp. 46-83

68. The first Bible in Albanian was published in 1824.

69. Naum Veqilharxhi (1797-1846)
One of the earliest figures to devote himself to the creation of the a new alphabet. One of the first Albanian nationalists. He died of poisoning in Constantinople.

70. J.G.V.Hahn (1811-1869)
The father of Albanology

71. Kostantin Kristoforidhi (1826-1895)
A leading figure of nineteenth century Albanian scholarship. He translated the Bible into Albanian. *See more in : Elsie, Vol.II. pp 131-132.*

72. Auguste Dozon (1822-1891)
French diplomat and scholar

73. Hasan Tahsini (1812-1881)
Albanian patriot from the south of Albania

74. Abdyl Bey Frasheri (1839-1892)
Leader of League of Prizren 1878

75. Prenk Bib Doda (1858-1920)
Leader of Mirdita in northern Albania

76. Mehmet Ali Vrioni (1842-1895)
A good friend of Abdyl Frasheri

77. League of Prizren (1878-1881)
An organisation of Albanian nationalists who opposed the Treaty of Berlin's decision to cede Albanian territory to Greece, Montenegro and Serbia. Their ambition was to form a greater Albania, comprising the four vilayets of Kosova, Scutari, Monastir and Yanina.

78. The Voice of Albania (1879-1880)
40 issues, edited by Anastas Kullurioti

79. Anastas Kullurioti(1822-1887)
Born in Athens of Albanian origin. Emigrated to USA and reportedly made his fortune there, he founded the weekly newspaper *'The Voice of Albania'*.

80. Nikolla Naço (1843-1913)
Acording to Konitza and Lasgush Poradec, Naço was the greatest Albanian patriot in Rumania. *See 'Lasgush Poradeci', Publicistika Tirane,1999.pp.144-320.*

81. Shkolla Shqipe e Vashave
An Albanian school established in Korce by Sevasti Qiriazi and her sister and brother

82. Avramidhi Lakçke
Albanian millionaire based in Rumania. He was elected the president of the independent Albanian colony in Bucharest.

83. Naim Bey Frasheri (1846-1900).
One of the greatest Albanian poets

84. Mehdi Bey Frashëri (1874-1963)
Writer, diplomat and statesman

85. Ismail Kemal Bey (1844-1919)
Great Albanian patriot and first president of Albania in 1912

86. Jorgji Meksi
Died in 1942. Acording to some Albanians, he is the father of Albanian journalism.

87. Thimi Mitko (1820-1890)
Great Albanian patriot, based in Cairo

88. Midhat Frashëri (1880-1949)
Great Albanian patriot, born in Yanina, Albanian Ambassador to Greece, President of Balli Kombëtar, poet and writer

INDEX

Albania 1,2,7,810,12,13,15,16,17, 18,20,23,26,26,32,325,44,47,48,49, 50,56,58,59,60,61,62,63,65,68,69, 70,74,76,79,81,84,88,89,90,93,94, 95,96,97,99,100,101,102,104,106, 109,110,111,112,113,114,115,117, 120,122,124,128,129,132,136,141, 146,147,147,1450,151,152,154,155, 161,163,164,165,166,167,168,168, 173,174,177,178,179
Albanians 7,8,11,12,14,15,17,19,25, 27,28,29,30,31,38,46,47,55,56,61, 62,70,71,72,79,86,98,99,104,105,10 7,
108,110,112,115,122,125,127,128, 129,134,139,147,148,153,154,155, 156,157,158,159.160,161,162,164, 166,168,170,171,174,175,176,178
Apollinaire,Guillaume 1
Ali Pasha 31,34,35
America 4,55

Bashkimi 48,51,,55
Bayle Pierre(1647-1706) (French/Dutch Lexicographer, philosopher and man of letters) 3
Bença, Shefqet 142
Berlin 66
Bismark, Otto von 72
Bogdani, Pjeter 1
Bourchier, J.D. 66
Boyle, Edward Sir (1878-1945) was the chairman of the Balkan Committee
Burney, Cecil, British Admiral (1858-1929). 64,65
Buxton,Noel (Lord Buxton 1869-1948) 122,123
Brussels 2

Cere,N 62
Cecil, Robert (Lord Robert Cecil) 115
Chekrezi, C 96 98, 101,113,102, 119,121, 123,130, 131,133
Cosenza 57
Dako Kristo 76
Dervish Bey Biçaku (Elbasani) 1 ,55, 57, 77, 81,
Dodani,Visarion,25,26,28,29,32,1 63,160
Duma, Dervish 117,120,121,127, 135
Duçi, Milo 170
Doda, Prenk Bib (also known as Prenk Pasha) 147
Durham, M Edith 58, 94, 97, 102, 112, 113, 122, 126
Dozon, Auguste 145

Faveyrial, Father 7
Fishta, Gjergj 60
Fitzmaurice, Edmond George (Lord Fitzmaurice) 60
France 1,7
Frashëri, Bey Abdyl 146,147, 148, 159
Frashëri, Alush 157
Frashëri, Bey Mehdi 159
Frashëri , Bey Mithat 159
Frasheëri, Bey Naim, 158
Frashëri, Bey Sami 152

Germany 66, 67, 68, 69, 70, 71
Giovanni, Alessandro 54
Giuliano [di] Marquis san 61,62
Goluchowski, Baron 14,18
Goschen, Lord 60
Goethe, J.W. von 71
Graham, Charlotte A. 141,143
Greece 61, 97
Greeks 10,11 ,34
Gurakuqi, Luigj 57

Hahn, J.G.von 145,149
Herbert, Aubrey 61,62, 63, 65, 81, 85
Herbert, Mary 81, 86
Hodgson, Robert Sir 112
Hull, Cordell 178

Ignatieff, Count,N.P 73
Ippen, Theodor 12
Ivanaj, Nikolla 53, 54, 56

Jagow, G.W. von 70
Jerome, Saint, 59

Kaçorri, Monsignor 59
Kastrati, Qazim 115
Kastrioti, Aladro,33
Kerran F.L 115
Konitza, Bey Faik 1,2,3,4,9,13,17,21,24, 25,27,28,29,33,36,38,39,42,42,49, 50,52,53,55,56,57,58,60,62,63,54, 65,67,68,75,76,80,83,84,85,89,90, 98,100,101,103,121,126,127,131, 132,133,134,135,136,138,140,141, 142,143,144,145,146,177
Konitza, Zejnel 34
Kosovo 10
Kulurioti A, 149
Kurti, Lec 104
Kristoforidhi, Kostantin 145

Lakçke, Avramidhi 155
Leake,William Martin 91
Logoreci, Anton 94,100,103,104, 112,113,118,123,135

Mackensen, A. von 71
Martini, Sotir 116,117,118,120,130, 131, 133,134,135,137,139,142,145
Meksi, Gjergj 164
Mommsen, Theodor 69,117,118, 119

Naçi, G.J. 131, 132, 134, 135, 136, 138, 144, 146, 179
Naco, Nikolla 149, 150, 151 152
Noli, F.S. 59, 96, 100,102
Nosi, Lef (1876-1945) 1, 57, 59

Oden, Robert 141,142

Pani, Vasil 131
Pekmezi, Gjergj 59
Percy, General 107, 114, 115, 121
Qiriazi, Gjergj 41
Qiriazi, Parashqevi 76

Robinson, Vandeleur 126

Sasvari, Armin 78

Sula, Abdyl 136
Toptani, Pashe Essad 65, 66
Toptani, Bey Murad 48, 151, 162
Tyko, Peter 142
Tzurani, S. 66
Vatra 82, 83, 84, 85, 101, 124, 126, 129, 139
Veqilharxhi, Naum 144
Vlora, Ismail Kemal Bey 162
Vrioni, Mehmet Ali 150

Welles, Sumner 102
Wied, W. von 66,68
Williams, Hattie 141

Xhuvani, Alexander 59

Zavalani, Tajar 94, 100, 103, 104, 112, 113
Zog, King 98,99,105,106,107,108, 113,114,115,116,117,118,121,122,1 23,126,127,130,131,132,133,13 4,135,136,137,138,140,143,145,
Zogolli, Pashe Xhemal 176
Zogolli, Pashe Gjelal,176

Acknowledgements

I am grateful to the following institutions and individuals for permission to publish the letters of Faik Konitza's:: the Albanian National Archive (AQSH) and its Director, Mr. Zamir Shtylla, Tirana, the Somerset Records Office (SRO), Mrs. Bridged Grant for permission to publish letters from Faik Konitza to her father (Aubrey Herbert), the Naçi Collection at the School of Slavonic and East European Studies (SSEES Naçi Collection), London, the Public Record Office, London, Mr. Alexander Duma for permission to use his father's collection which is cited under the Dervish Duma Archive at the Centre for Albanian Studies (DDA,CAS), the American Pan-Albanian organisation Vatra, its journal *'Dielli'* and its president Mr. Agim Karagjozi and Mr. Gjekë Gjonlekaj of the Gjonlekaj Publishing Company based in New York.

My depest gratitude is due to my translators: Harry Hodgkinson, Mandy Belster, Peter Rennie, Robert Elsie, Paulin Kola and Andrea Lesic.

I am also grateful to Noel Malcolm and Professor Harry Norris for their helpful comments and suggestions, and as always to Westrow Cooper.

This book was initiated and supported by the following friends and admirers of Konitza: Florie Sefaj, Teuta Skenderi, Akil Koci, Avdul Gula, Emin Ratkoceri, Burim Bytyqi, Ilir Venhari, Ilir Havolli, F. Nikaj and Arben Damani.

For assistance with IT and design, I would like to thank Eddie, Tony and Graham at Learning Design and Sylejman Pashoja, Ilir Hamiti, Agim Morina and Driton Tali.

B.D.
December 2000

Errata

On page viii, the last line has been inadvertently omitted. It should read *'...awarded to Greece.'*

'Turkish' is mispelt in the caption on the inside back cover.